MOVE

MOUNTAINS

HOW TO ACHIEVE ANYTHING IN YOUR LIFE WITH THE POWER OF POSITIVE THINKING

R.L. Adams

R.L. ADAMS

This Page Intentionally Left Blank

From The

Inspirational Books Series

by

R.L. Adams

- *Breakthrough – Live an Inspired Life, Overcome your Obstacles and Accomplish your Dreams*

- *Have a Little Hope – An Inspirational Guide to Discovering What Hope is and How to have More of it in your Life*

- *How Not to Give Up – A Motivational & Inspirational Guide to Goal Setting & Achieving your Dreams*

- *How to be Happy – An Inspirational Guide to Discovering What Happiness is and How to have More of it in your Life*

- *Move Mountains – How to Achieve Anything in your Life with the Power of Positive Thinking*

- *The Silk Merchant – Ancient Words of Wisdom to Help you Live a Better Life Today*

This Page Intentionally Left Blank

CONTENTS

R.L. ADAMS

This Page Intentionally Left Blank

INTRODUCTION

"That's been one of my mantras - focus and simplicity. Simple can be harder than complex: You have to work hard to get your thinking clean to make it simple. But it's worth it in the end because once you get there, you can move mountains." — Steve Jobs

I used to be stuck in the past. Although I don't care much for the past anymore, I used to live and dwell there. I used to be fixated on the former events of my life, replaying them over, and over in my head, vividly, as though they were broken projection reels set for perpetual play in the theater of my mind. I can still recall today how intensely I would sit in that theater. Sometimes I would be in the front row sobbing. Other times I was seated in the middle of the dark empty theater, dead center, with my fists rolled up into balls, mentally unleashing bouts of rage that seemed to come from nowhere. And sometimes, when I entered that theater, I would sit depressed in the very back row, watching the movie reels with a distant longing, as the unsteady picture flickered on and off, clouding the fading memories into nothingness.

The theater of my mind was always open. I always felt like a patron that was confined to that theater, unable to escape. I wasn't living in the present. I was stuck in the past, and I couldn't seem to get unstuck. I couldn't find my way past all the hurt and the pain. I couldn't look beyond the agony that I had suffered, the betrayals that were done, and the words that were said. I was tormented by the emotions of pain, fear, guilt, anxiety, and worry. But I was tired of living that life. I was tired of waking up every single day feeling devoid of pure joy. I wanted to be free, but I was trapped, as if all the exits to that theater in my mind were locked shut with thick ironclad chains and unbreakable padlocks. I felt like I couldn't get free.

I'm not sure what happened after that. Maybe you can call it a spiritual awakening, or maybe you can call it some form of *self*-actual realization, but whatever it was, it was powerful. And it was almost as if the level of noise came to this crescendo, that then cracked my ego from my inner self. And when I talk about the ego, I really am almost referring to someone else – still a part of me, but someone entirely different, or at least that's how it felt anyways. That's because the ego shrouds so much for the subconscious mind and hides the true inner self. The ego acts as a barrier, protecting the inner self from any hurt or external pain that it may suffer due to the cause of others. It seeks to protect the inner self from that, but it also ends up hiding the true inner self from really shining through. My ego was hard at work protecting my very fragile inner self. It was hard at work, trying every which way to ensure that the world outside couldn't pierce its heavily armored shell.

The subconscious mind and the ego work together with one another, acting in collusion – and that's just what they did to me. They worked to produce certain thoughts, and feed certain emotions that kept me feeling trapped in their inner wrangling. But everyone experiences this. Everyone goes through the self-defeating emotional rollercoaster ride that has you spinning inside your own head. You know the kind I'm talking about right? The kind that leaves you feeling empty, desolate, isolated, fearful, worrisome, and anxious inside. It wreaks havoc on you. It tortures you, incessantly creating a never-ending series of self-deprecating patterns of thoughts, emotions and resultant behaviors that perpetually puts you on edge. Yes, this happened to me, and it happened for a long time.

One day though, I awakened. I came to see what I hadn't seen before – I saw the error of my ways, and began to watch the bouts that my ego and inner self had in the fighting ring of my mind. I wasn't trapped in that theater anymore. I could move mountains. I was free. I was free from the mental prison that had me living in the past, reliving old tormented events, and reviving all but dead feelings that should have stayed in the very distant past. It was liberating. I was no longer trapped in the pressure cooker of life that had me clinging for air. I was no longer a mental, spiritual, physical, or emotional slave to the battles being waged in my mind, or playing out on the screens of its theater.

When I talk about it now, it truly does feel like I'm talking about someone else's life. I feel like I'm talking about someone else's past. But it was my own. Not only was it my own, it was a very big part of me back then. It was huge in fact. It forced me to create enormous amounts of internal strife that didn't allow me to progress and move past the tumult. Back then, I didn't feel like I could accomplish any goal, achieve any dream, or move any mountain. I couldn't do any of that because I wasn't free. I needed to be free of the feelings that haunted me and forced me to wage wars against my inner self on a constant basis. I couldn't stop the bullets from ricocheting inside my mind until I extricated my true inner self. But this freedom of my inner self came at a huge cost in my life. It came at the cost of nearly everything that I had once cherished, and everything I had once ever known. I had to give it all up and start all over, but it didn't have to be that way.

The understanding that I reached didn't have to be so difficult — I just chose it to be that way. I was stubborn. I was so wrapped up in the past that I couldn't see beyond it. I couldn't see beyond the events, the mishaps, and the failures. I was literally blinded by the past. And before this period of time that involved the freedom of my inner self from my ego, I suffered through extended bouts of suicidal depression. Amongst all the other angst that I was faced with, it all seemed to peak until things came crashing down around me. The window of falseness cracked and shattered, and the feeling of a veil being lifted off my face came over me. I felt a stillness in my mind that I hadn't felt before, and an overall sense of ease I hadn't experienced prior to that in my life, and it was profound to say the least. But beyond the quietude that washed over me, I was able to come to a deep understanding about why I wanted the things I truly wanted, and how I could get them.

I experienced a mental shift in this period. I moved from a life of just wanting, to a life of expecting. I moved from wishing, to commanding. I was able to achieve my dreams, conquer my demons, and accomplish my goals. I was able to move mountains. I felt like I could literally accomplish anything I put my mind to, and so can you. And that phrase "Move Mountains," has an utterly deep and profound meaning. It has a meaning that's rooted not only in Biblical terms as is seen in Matthew 17:20, "Because you have so little faith. Truly I tell you, if you have faith as small as a mustard seed, you can say to this mountain, 'Move from here to there,' and it will move.

Nothing will be impossible for you." But the phrase is also rooted in modern-day success theory and humankind's undying quest to overcome insurmountable obstacles, and accomplish seemingly impossible feats, all in the face of great adversity with the singular weapon of the powerful mind. I wanted to be able to move mountains, and I could.

But the ability to move mountains isn't just some historical folklore. It isn't just something found in fantasy fiction novels, or only achievable by people with seemingly super powers. No, the ability to move mountains lies within each of us. The ability to be able to conquer our goals, achieve our dreams, and push through the present-day limitations imposed upon us, lies within us all. It's locked up inside the mind, quarantined by the ego from our inner selves. "I can't achieve something," is the lie that exists due to the ego trying to protect our inner selves. It's trying to protect us with that fragile film that surrounds the inner self, that's so quickly shattered and torn when we're faced with the slightest failure or criticism. But when you learn to embrace failure and use it to fuel you rather than defeat you, you can truly move mountains. You can accomplish anything.

I'm sure you've heard that phrase before, "Move Mountains." I know I had. But I never really understood it. I never really understood what it took to come to this understanding about how my mind can work against me, and stop me from really achieving the things I wanted in my life. I didn't want to believe or know about the inner wrangling happening in my mind. And when I learned that this is a defense mechanism created by the ego to help mask and hide this inner wrangling, it all started to make a little bit more sense to me. It all started to come together when I realized all the complexity at work in the mind that forces us to be at odds with our inner selves. If you've ever felt anxious, worried, or fearful about your future, you're not alone. You're not alone because that's part of the mind's self-defense mechanisms. It's at odds with itself – it's trying to protect that fragile inner self that lies within you. It's trying to protect it from all the hurt and the pain it can potentially suffer.

In reaching this understanding, and building an awareness for the way my mind operates, I was able to point my mind in the right direction. I was able to implant certain programming in my mind that would push me to achieve the things I always wanted to achieve, but was too scared to do in the past. And it can help you too. It can help you to come to the understanding that you've been longing for. It can help ease the anxiety and worry in your mind once and for all. It can help you set out and accomplish your dreams by being more present than ever before. And this understanding can help to align you with your true inner thoughts and dreams, without the shrouded protection of the ego, and the falsity that it tends to throw up as glass walls to protect its fragile inner self.

You know the saying, "Knowledge is power," and it couldn't be truer in this instance. Because throughout the years, people have accomplished extraordinary feats, all in the face of great adversity – they have moved mountains. Records have been broken, technology has been invented, and innovation has quickened at breakneck speeds, all in the name of progress. Progress that wasn't easily achieved, but it happened when we learned to break the mold and move those mountains. So, if you've been faced with a challenge in your past and haven't been able to move mountains, this book is for you. If you've been overcome by the mental disquietude that we all experience on a regular basis, blocking the ability to successfully tackle obstacles, this book is for you. If you've been feeling an uneasiness, and an inability to pinpoint your deep-rooted problems, then this book is for you. This book is for you if you want to move mountains, whatever those mountains may be in your own life.

1
THE BIG PICTURE

"Human progress is neither automatic nor inevitable... Every step toward the goal of justice requires sacrifice, suffering, and struggle; the tireless exertions and passionate concern of dedicated individuals." – Martin Luther King Jr.

On a hot summer day in the late 12th century, in the remote outskirts of the French Pyrenees village town, St. Jean Pied de Port, a group of people gathered to make an 800-kilometer pilgrimage across Northern Spain called the Camino de Santiago, or the Way of St. James. The journey, which winds its way around the Pyrenees Mountains and through numerous villages dotted along the Northern Coast of Spain, takes about one month to complete. It ends at the Cathedral of Santiago de Compostela, in Northwest Spain. The final destination in Santiago de Compostela is the burial place of the Apostle, Saint James.

The first pilgrimages began in the 9th century after a

hermit by the name of Pelayo, discovered the tomb. He was led by a vision to the remote burial site that enshrined one of the twelve original Apostles. It was hailed as an incredible find, and just what Spain needed to help inspire its citizens and people around the world in the name of Christianity. Back then, the Moors were invading Spain, and the discovery (or rediscovery) in the 9th century happened at the most opportune time to help motivate the Spaniards against the invading forces.

The pilgrimages to Santiago de Compostela started shortly after the discovery in the 9th century, and over the centuries, many people have walked the Camino to pay their respects at the burial site of the Apostle. The frequency of pilgrimages started small, but word quickly spread throughout Spain, France, Italy, and across the entire European continent. People began traveling from everywhere to reach the remote route, and the entire journey has taken on a very meaningful experience for the individual that decided to head out and walk the Camino. Today, over one million people make the journey every year.

But in the late 12th century, this particular group of pilgrims made their way out onto the Camino just as many had done before them. Each person in the group started out with a specific reason in their minds as to why they were making the journey. For the past few hundred years before them, pilgrims would walk the Camino with the clear intent as to why they were doing it. Each of them had emblazoned a purpose for their journey. Some did it for religious reasons, while others used the Camino as more of tool for self-discovery.

Claudio, one of the pilgrims in the late 12th century group, was doing it for religious reasons, while Peter, was on a mission to find himself. All of the men and women in the group came from various different backgrounds from across Europe. Some in the group were merchants who peddled their wares in street markets, while others were blacksmiths, artisans, and farmers. But they all had one singular common thread – they were all on a unique personal journey, and the Camino had a particular meaning to them in their hearts.

The group met that summer day at the origin of their journey in St. John Pied de Port. The small French town stands at the base of the Roncevaux Pass across the Pyrenees, and at first, they were but random strangers who had all picked the same day to start their Camino. As they made their way along the route, some spoke, while others walked silently. Some prayed during their journey, while others just soaked up the quiet, tranquil landscape and surroundings, along the way. After the first few days of walking, the group came around a bend along the Pyrenees Mountain Pass to find a group of stonecutters who were working away chipping at stones. They could see them from a distance. Half of the men were sitting down, while the other half were toiling away working in the field at the base of the mountain, but none of the men seemed happy about what they were doing. Some were working harder than others, but it was clear that the arduous task they were engaged in, was taking a severe toll on them under the hot summer sun.

"Hello there. What are you men doing?" Asked the outspoken, Claudio, who silently elected himself to be the leader of the group. The stonecutters, who were working, stopped what they were doing long enough to grimace at the group of pilgrims making their way along the route. Feeling uneasy, the group decided to continue walking by as a tall muscular man with a thick black beard glared the pilgrims down just long enough to quip, "Why, what does it look like we're doing here? We're cutting stone in this terrible heat, of course." And with that response, the pilgrims continued with their journey.

A week later, as they made their way across Northern Spain, the pilgrims happened upon another group of men who were also working away cutting and chipping stone. This group was similar to the first group of stonecutters. Their grimaced looks were a clear indication that they weren't happy with their predicament as well. The unapproachable stonecutters paid no attention to the pilgrims as both groups ignored each other, and the pilgrims walked by silently, heads bowed low.

Finally, on their last day of the journey, as they reached the final resting place of the Apostle St. James, they happened upon another group of stonecutters. But this group of men was different. All of the men were working while smiling, joking, and laughing. There wasn't even one of them who was sitting down, and they didn't make anyone feel uncomfortable. In fact, the pilgrims could see the whites of the stonecutters' smiling teeth as they came closer and closer to the men, something that was rare to find amongst men working hard labor in the hot summer sun. But based on their past two experiences, the group of pilgrims were still wary of interacting with this group of stonecutters for fear of being chided again. But as they neared the tomb of the Apostle St. James and came closer to the pillar that had been erected in his honor, Peter, a merchant from Rome, waved at the group and smiled.

"Hello," said Peter.

"Well hello," said the man who looked to be the foreman of the small clan hammering away. He yelled at them from a distance, but came running over to greet the group as they gathered around the stone pillar.

"It's a very hot day for stonecutting, wouldn't you say?" Peter said it with a big smile on his face, as the smiles on the group of stonecutters' faces were contagious.

The stonecutter reached out his hand to greet each of the pilgrims that had arrived. "I'm Bernardo and, yes, well of course it is. But, we're not just cutting stone here," said the man in return.

Peter looked at his group of pilgrims, then to Claudio with a puzzled look on his face. Claudio chimed in, "Well, what is it that you men are doing then? It clearly looks like you're cutting stone like the last few groups of men we saw along the Camino."

"Well," the foreman said in return, this time smiling an even wider smile, "Like those other men, and the many other groups of men commissioned to cut stone along the Camino, we are doing much more than merely cutting stone. You see, we're building a cathedral in honor of St. James. It will be called the Cathedra of Santiago de Compostela, and it will be the most glorious cathedral in all of Spain. We are more than just stonecutters, we are cathedral builders, and we've been entrusted with the most important work in all of Spain. It may seem like just stonecutting to the other men, who are working on this same task, but to us, we are chipping away little by little to someday finally build something great." And with that the foreman smiled, waved then ran back off to continue working under the hot Spanish sun.

*****

People have a tendency to see the obstacles standing in their ways differently. For some, the obstacles are merely temporary, and they know that with consistent daily effort, they will overcome those obstacles. They can see the bigger picture of just what the obstacles truly mean to them. They can appreciate that the obstacles will make them stronger, wiser, and faster. It will help them grow, mature, and to become better people. Even in the face of failure, they use those obstacles to learn more, be more, and achieve more. They use them as a platform for moving to the next level in life. They are the type of people that know what it means to achieve something. They know what sacrifices are involved with achieving something worthwhile. They know just what it takes to overcome their obstacles, and instead of fixating themselves on those obstacles, they remained focused on their goals. And they know that any goal worthwhile isn't only about the destination, it's about who you become during the journey. That journey couldn't help to mold and shape them without those obstacles. Those obstacles make them better people – they define them.

Yet, most people are very disturbed by obstacles. They are disturbed by the effort that it takes to overcome obstacles that remain in their paths. They are disturbed by the amount of sacrifice it's going to take to overcome those obstacles. They think of all the sleepless nights, the emotional pains, and the long hours of work it will take to achieve their goals. They begin to think of all the reasons why their obstacles are so big, and so insurmountable, that eventually they become just that. Initially, they're excited by their goals. Initially, they feel like they will overcome their obstacles in a half-hearted fashion. They generally tend to give a big push to get things off the ground, but unlike the achievers, their efforts wax and wane, while the excitement of the new goal begins to wear off. Then, they reach a plateau; they're lured by temptations, and eventually, resign from their goals just as fast as they had begun them. They just give up.

But the quitters set out the same as the achievers. They start out the same way as the people who see obstacles as mere mental blockades that are overcome with time, patience, and hard work. In the beginning, the quitters are just as excited by the task, as the achievers are. They are excited by the possibility and potential to achieve their new goals. They think about how great it would feel to achieve those goals, and just how fulfilling and satisfying it would be. But there's a big difference. The quitters seem to lack the ability to follow through. They seem to lack the spirit to give it all they have. Something just doesn't compute for them, and they revert to their old patterns and behaviors. They give up their goals at the slightest sign of resistance. When they realize just how much work and effort it's going to take, they throw in the towel, and mentally, emotionally, physically, and spiritually shut down. They just give up.

But giving up is easy to do. It's easy to just want to quit something when you begin to come to grips with the amount of effort moving that mountain is going to take. It's easy to allow the immensity of a goal to overwhelm and overtake you. It's easy for that to happen. And it's easy to throw your hands up in the air in silent resignation when the going gets tough. It's easy to lay down your arms and surrender to the obstacle that's once again defeated you. It's easy to succumb to the pain and the anguish that's placed on you in the face of adversity. It's easy to look up at that mountain looming over you and feel its oppressive nature bearing down on you, taunting you. It's easy to just give up.

So, what makes the achievers and the quitters so different? How is it that one person can set their mind on something, and push through any obstacle standing in their way, while the other can quit at the slightest sign of resistance? What makes the difference between someone who, no matter how many times they have to fail, continues their drive in the pursuit of their goals? What's the difference between these people? So much. So much is the difference between these people. And if you've ever set goals and really achieved them, you know just what it takes. You know just how much sacrifice is required of you. You know just how many sleepless nights and long hours of work it takes to achieve your hopes and your dreams.

But the problem is, most people don't want to put in the work. Most people want the instant gratification of achieving major goals that are difficult, without all the effort. Most people are just set in their ways. It's difficult to push through and overcome an obstacle, and pursue a hope, or a dream, when you're not used to the immensity of spirit, drive, and determination required to achieve something worthwhile. We live in an instant gratification society. From fast food, to fad diets, and get-rich-quick schemes, people want what they want, and they want it now. And the unfortunate truth is that the mainstream media doesn't help to quell this desire for immediate satisfaction. Everything is now, now, now, and we lack the patience truly required to achieve things worthwhile.

But goals can be hard like that. And goals can be incredibly hard when they're combined with all of the other stresses and commitments that exist in life. Goals can be hard when there are so many more things that need to be worried about. And goals can become undone, when other major problems or calamity strikes. When something else bad happens in your life, it just seems like all of it piles on together to make this one giant mess of insurmountable obstacles. A ripple effect occurs, affecting everything in its wake. It can get overwhelming for anyone, but we all know that accomplishing real goals that are worthwhile means a lot more than just a quick and simple push of effort. You have to be in it for the long haul. You have to persist and persevere, even when everything inside of you is screaming to just give up.

Goals are powerful any way you look at them. Whether

they're beckoning you to achieve, or questioning your entire existence, goals can make or break you. They can help fuel the fire in the furnace of hope. They are what set the pedal to the metal, and when combined with action, they can help you to produce enormous results in your life. Results you would have never thought you could once achieve. From Thomas Edison, to Henry Ford, to Steve Jobs, and everyone in between, goals fueled the fire in the furnace of hope for them. But unlike many others who decided to give up in the world, they were able to materialize their goals with action and perseverance. They were able to see their goals come to fruition. They didn't allow the goals to break them. They allowed the goals to define them.

But achieving major goals like that doesn't come easy. It isn't easy to push through the pain and the anguish that it takes to achieve any notable success. It isn't easy to set your goals and achieve them on a consistent basis. It just isn't easy. And those goals can make you begin to question your entire being. "Am I good enough for this?" You may ask, or "Can I really do this?" You begin to call into question your mental, physical, emotional, and spiritual faculties. You begin to doubt. You begin to doubt whether or not you can really move that mountain. You begin to doubt that you could ever achieve that goal, that hope, or that dream. You begin to doubt everything that you once thought you believed in. You begin to doubt everything, question everything, and second-guess everything. But there's a big difference between, thinking you believe you can do something, and knowing you believe you can do something. There's a big difference between making something a "should," as opposed to making something a "must." When you believe, truly and wholeheartedly in yourself, and in your goals, it's a must. It's always a must. It has to be a must. And when it's a must you can truly move any mountain. There's a very big difference there.

But for most people, goals aren't a must. The sad truth is that most people look at goals as only something they "should" do. If the goals were a must, nothing would stand in their way. And we've all had goals that have been both *shoulds* and *musts*. We've all had the experience of setting our eyes on something, and achieving it no matter what. But, then again, we've also all had the experience of wanting something, but then quitting in a half-hearted effort that stopped just as quick as it started. We've all reached that point where we began pushing and pushing towards that goal to move that mountain, and we hit a wall. Some of us hit a very large wall, having to toil away relentlessly to move the blockage from the path to our goals. For the weak spirit, these walls can crush goals. They can act as an impenetrable fortress to achievement, a locked safe with no key, or an impossible puzzle to solve. But, for others, these walls define people, and it's these types of walls, that success is made from. These are the walls that differentiate the talkers from the doers. These are the walls that can be slowly chipped away at, like the stonecutter cutting away at the rock, taking away a little bit each time until finally, the stone gives way, the safe unlocks, the fortress unveils itself, the puzzle is solved, and the mountain is moved.

Life is full of these walls. It's full of walls that seem to mystically appear as barriers to our goals. It's full of walls that seem to be so impenetrable at first, to the weak and untrained spirit. Life is made of these walls, and these walls are what make moving those mountains so entirely difficult. They act as life's obstacle course, appearing everywhere you turn and look. As you push, life throws more walls at you, working tirelessly to defeat you. It seemingly does everything in its might to cut you back down to size, and see you become just another talker. So, is this some sort of achievement trap? Are we destined to keep hitting life's walls, never to truly fulfill our hopes, our dreams, and our goals? Are we never to be able to move those mountains that stand in the pathway to our success?

Well, we all know that in this world, nothing comes easy. Nothing is simple to achieve that's truly worth achieving. It takes work. It takes hard work, and it takes time. But most people aren't willing to do the work or put in the time that's required to achieve something notable. Most people want to just escape back into their old pleasure-driven habits rather than focus on their goals. When you don't want something bad enough, distractions are only a moment away. It's easy to kick up your feet and relax, especially if you begin hitting that wall. It's easy to stop working so hard, especially when you reach a plateau. And major goals aren't reached right away, because they usually involve hitting several walls, and several plateaus. They usually involve running into wall after wall after wall, falling down multiple times, repeatedly. But all of this makes it difficult to know when the end is in sight. It makes it difficult to see the forest through the trees when you can barely see past the bushes.

If you've heard the saying, "Good things come to those who wait," it's true to a degree. It should more likely be, "Good things come to those who work hard, and wait," because moving mountains involves a lot of hard work, and a lot of waiting. It can get incredibly frustrating at times, especially when you don't see the fruits of your labors right away. It can also involve many failures. You're going to fail many times before you achieve that goal and you move those mountains. But life's full of these failures. It's full of setbacks that knock you off your feet, take the air from your lungs, and seemingly cut you back down to size. It can get frustrating for anyone. Anyone.

But no one ever said life was going to be easy. No one ever said life was going to be a walk in the park. No one ever said you were going to be able to live on easy street, without first slumming it through skid row. Nothing worthwhile is going to come easy. Nothing is going to be handed to you on a silver platter. But if you're going to move those mountains, overcome those obstacles, or achieve your hopes, and your dreams, it all boils down to just one thing – your beliefs. If you believe it can happen, and it's a must for you, it will. But I'm not talking about the kind of outward belief that we think we may have at times. I'm talking about true inner belief. I'm talking about the kind of belief that's a burning passion that fuels the fire of your dreams, and keeps the flame of hope alive always. That's what life's all about. That's what separates the doers from the talkers.

2

THE POWER OF BELIEFS

"One life is all we have and we live it as we believe in living it. But to sacrifice what you are and to live without belief, that is a fate more terrible than dying." — Joan of Arc

Alistair looked in the mirror. The thirty-four year old media executive ran his hand through his hair, quickly checking his complexion as he finished getting ready for work. He had been anxiously waiting for this day, and it couldn't have come any sooner. He was going to be promoted to Senior VP of Programming; he could just feel it. It was a day he had been tirelessly working towards for the past 10 years. Nothing had come easy. None of it was a walk in the park. From the moment he left college 13 years ago, to the very first day he started with the Network, through to the present day, he had worked and sweated his butt off in the corporate media world. He bowed down, kissed toes, and brown-nosed to every single person he had to, all while also keeping his nose to the grindstone, avoiding conflict, and slowly moving up the corporate ladder.

The first employee in the office each day, and the last employee to leave in the evening, there was no one that deserved the promotion more than Alastair. "Senior VP of Programming," he said to himself as he smiled at the near-perfectly-whitened teeth smiling back at him in the reflection. "Today is your day," he said again as he shut the car door and backed out of the garage on his way to work. This was the day. Finally, it was here. All he could think about was the blood, sweat, tears, and long hours, he had put in for the Network. All he could think about was how much he had sacrificed just to be their all-star executive. Nothing had come easy. Nothing.

On the drive into work, Alastair's thoughts ran a mile-a-minute. His stream of consciousness was going haywire. The morning news was playing on the radio, but he was almost completely unaware of it. The self-talk in his mind was on overdrive. "What if I don't get that promotion?" As the single negative thought somehow invaded his mind, it snowballed into feelings of angst and fear. He couldn't allow himself to think that way. No, he was going to get the promotion. He was sure of it. "But... what if?" The what-ifs started running through his mind. "What if I'm passed up again? What then?" He didn't want to think of that, but he couldn't help but think of it. It was almost as if the more he told himself he wouldn't think of it, the more he did.

After driving through the midtown tunnel, and finally emerging on the other side in the heart of New York City, his senses came alive. The tunnel was the calm before the storm. In the tunnel, it was dead silent except for the repetitive swoosh sounds from the joints in the tunnel road that was violently disrupted by a city that was humming on the other end. Buses hissing, cars honking, people shuffling, and steam rising from grates – there was nothing like it in his mind. As Alistair battled the mid-town maze to get to the corporate headquarters of the Network, he ran the different scenarios in his mind. What would he do if he didn't get the promotion? Would it be time for a change? After so many years at the same Network, would it be safe to change now? What if he couldn't actually land another job? He began to worry.

The trip up the elevator felt like it would take forever. It was D-Day in his mind. With the looming potential of the promotion, Alastair knew the day was going to drag on forever. Would his boss let him know today? Kenneth, the old Senior VP of Programming's last day, was Friday. It was Monday. He had to find out today. They still hadn't announced anything. He began to wind himself up again. What if? It felt like his insides were fighting with one another. "It doesn't matter," he kept trying to tell himself, but he kept feeling anxious, worried and afraid he wouldn't get the promotion.

The office was still quiet. None of the executive staff had started to shuffle in yet, and Alastair's boss was nowhere to be found. He usually waltzed in shortly after 9am, but that was still a couple of hours away. Alastair checked his email to find no new news. "Now what?" He couldn't work. He couldn't concentrate. He couldn't do anything but think of that promotion. More what-ifs ran through his mind, and then he decided that that was going to be it. He wasn't going to think about it anymore. He would deal with it when he found out. But his insides were tearing themselves apart yearning to know the answer. He was screaming out onto a deaf world, but no one could hear him. No one knew what he had sacrificed. No one knew what he had been through – the torture he had put himself through. It was hard. It was more than hard in fact – it was nearly impossible.

But, Alistair believed in himself. He believed beyond any doubt, that he would succeed. He really didn't leave himself any choice. As an orphan, Alistair bounced around from foster home to foster home, and never really had a chance to have a real home. He didn't want that for his own kids, and he swore to himself that, when he did have kids one day, that they would have a stable family home to always come back to. He created strong enough reasons why he had to succeed; there was no turning back. He believed so strongly in himself and his abilities that, he wasn't going to let anything stop him. He promised himself he would work hard to achieve his goals, and it was finally starting to pay off. All the long hours, grueling work, and frequent setbacks were finally going to pay off.

Alistair lost himself in his thoughts for a few minutes. Time stood still as he weighed the accomplishments in his mind. It was a wonderful feeling. He couldn't feel more proud of anything else he had done in his entire life. He had made a difference. He had achieved so much in such a short period. And, he hadn't worker for anything else in his life. Against all odds, somehow he saw himself through it all. Somehow, he had the will and the tenacity, to buck the trend of misaligned youths who exit the foster care system. He was considered an anomaly; he was one of the lucky ones. But to him, it was simple. It wasn't luck. It was an undying belief that he could, he would, and he must succeed. That was it.

As the office staff shuffled in that morning, Alistair smiled to himself. He knew what he had done. He knew what he had accomplished, and how much of himself he had given. He knew it deep down inside, in his heart of hearts. And when his boss shuffled past his office, he gave a quick glance in through the glass windows and smiled. He smiled that smile that one would smile only when there was exceedingly good news. He knocked on the window, and stood in the doorway. "Alistair. Can you come out here for a minute?"

"Sure, what's up?" Alistair knew what was up, but he didn't want to sound conceited about it.

Michael, the President of the Network, pulled him into the center of the room where all the cubicles were located, and he started to speak. Alistair's face turned flush red. "People. I have an announcement to make. The first thing I want to say is that Patricia will be the new Senior VP of Programming."

Alistair's heart stopped. "What! Oh no!" He went from bright red to white. All the blood seemed to rush out of his system leaving him looking white as a ghost. They were all staring at him now. "Oh no. Now what?" He just wanted to scream!

"And I also want to say," continued his boss, "that Alistair here will be the new Vice President of the entire Network. You will all be reporting to him now." He turned to look at Alistair. "Son, you deserve this more than anyone I could possibly think of. Congratulations on all the hard work."

Alistair was shocked. He didn't know what was going on. He felt embarrassed and elated all at the same time. "Sir, thank you. I can't tell you how much I..."

Michael cut him off as he was speaking. "Like I said, there's no one else who deserves this more than you. Congratulations. You'll be my number two in charge of the whole Network from now on." He reached out to shake Alistair's hand. It was the proudest he had ever felt in his entire life.

"Thank you, sir. You won't regret this. Thank you."

*****

There's something so powerful about deep-rooted beliefs. There's something so powerful about knowing, in your heart-of-hearts, that you can accomplish something. There's something just so powerful about that. There's something so moving and so compelling about a person who can struggle, in the face of all adversity, and overcome their obstacles. There's something so endearing to us that, no matter how many times we hear the stories of people overcoming huge adversity to persevere, we're touched by it. That's because people love the story of an underdog. They love to see a person who can push through their obstacles, defeat their demons, and move their mountains. That's what dreams are made of.

But to do all that, you have to be able to adapt to life, and the many things that it throws at you. You have to be able to remain steadfast, even when everyone else seems to be losing his or her cool. You have to be able to have the mental, spiritual, emotional, and physical fortitude that's required of people who want to accomplish anything formidable in life. You have to be able to persevere, and believe that you can accomplish anything, do anything, go anywhere, and be anyone. You have to have the power of true inner belief in yourself, in order to tackle life's ever-changing ways. You have to be able to roll with the punches, and adjust your approach as life throws its curveballs at you.

But we all know that life is full of change. It's full of change that's happening all around us at every moment in time. It's full of changes that make us scream aloud. It's full of changes that make us cry tears of joy, or weep tears of sorrow. It's full of a lot of different change, all the time. From the small changes happening on a cellular level in all organic living things, to the larger changes happening on a macro level across environments, societies, and economies. Life and all of its components are relentlessly changing every moment of the day. And our bodies have been built to constantly create, analyze, and adapt to that change. Through the billions of neurons in your brain sending out neurotransmissions to make your body function autonomously, along with the ability for you to think, analyze, and make decisions, change is a core component of life.

Change is constant, but learning to adapt to change can be difficult, especially if you're not accustomed to external change. Even though change is happening all around you, and within your physical makeup each moment of the day, you may not be adapt to change on a larger scale. That's because change can be uncomfortable for most people. It adds a level of uncertainty to people's lives. It creates havoc where there is peace, it can create anxiety where people are stress-free, and it can force you to alter familiar patterns and habits that are hard to break. This type of change – the kind that can uproot you from your very existence – can be very difficult to accept.

It can be hard to summon up the level of adaptation to change required to succeed at your goals in life. It can be hard to wake up and appreciate change for what it is – something that helps you grow and mature. It's oftentimes hard to see the good in change. We usually look at change as suspect and foreign. We usually don't like it when change enters our lives, when the familiarity of things around us begins to shift. That's because we are creatures of habits. Most of us are set in our ways, and used to our patterns. We drive the same route to work, eat the same things for lunch, and watch the same types of television programs and movies. But external change is happening all around us, and if you're going to succeed at your goals, you must learn to adapt to external change, even if it's out of your comfort zone.

You may not be accustomed to external change. You may not be accustomed to uprooting your behaviors and habits in a way that requires high adaptability when it's unnecessary. I'm not talking about forced change here, or the kind that's placed on you involuntarily. That kind of change would include the loss of a job, a house, a spouse, an income, or some other drastic type of change that would force you to have to adapt. When change like that happens, you have no choice but to adapt. If you can't adapt, you can't survive. It's as simple as that. I'm not talking about involuntary change, because that type of change is straightforward. You have no choice but to have to adapt to that kind of change.

What I'm talking about is voluntary change. Voluntary change, or change in yourself for the better, is difficult for most people to adapt to. It's difficult for most people to follow through on voluntary changes that need to be done in their lives in order to achieve the goals they want to achieve. It's difficult for most people to decide, in the first place, what they need to change, and then actually make the efforts to change it. It's difficult for most people to follow through on change like this. It's difficult to have an eagle's eye, be laser-focused on your goals, and do what you need to do in order to achieve them. Most of us are so used to having things being dictated to us that it's hard to see what needs to be done on our own. We might know in the back of our minds what we have to do, but we usually lack the wherewithal to do it.

And people are resistant to change. They're resistant to changes that will interrupt the behavior that they've become so accustomed to. It's certainly hard to teach an old dog new tricks, especially when the tricks they already have, help to create more of that emotion-numbing activity that allows them to avoid seeing that change in the first place. It's hard to allow yourself to find new and improved ways to live your life, and carry out your pursuits, in the direction of your dreams. It's easy to get quickly discouraged and not follow through. It's easy to be resistant to change because most of us require structure and certainty, and without structure and certainty, we feel lost. But you can't be resistant to change if you're going to accomplish your goals. You can't be resistant to change if you're going to fulfill your hopes, and your dreams. And you can't be resistant to change if you're going to move mountains. It just won't work.

But if you can't adapt to change, both involuntary and voluntary, you can't survive. You can't survive when it comes to involuntary change that's thrust upon you without your consent. You can't adapt to life if you lose your job, your house, your car, or any other tools affecting your ability to earn and produce income. But you have no choice, because if you can't adapt to involuntary change, you can't survive. And in turn, if you can't adapt to voluntary change, you can't thrive. You may survive living life on an average level, but you'll never thrive. It's that plain and simple. And human beings were meant to thrive. We were meant to achieve any goal, dream, or hope that we set out to achieve in life. We were meant not only adapt to change, but also to embrace it. You must embrace change in every form, from the physical, to the emotional, to the mental, to the financial, and to the spiritual, in order to thrive. It's this type of change, on a grand level, that's required to achieve your goals. This is the type of massive change required that will allow you to move mountains.

Without embracing voluntary change in your life, how could a person lose weight for example? Losing weight involves such an all-encompassing change to one's voluntary behaviors and habits – both internal and external – that it affects every aspect of their lives. When you want to lose weight, you need to start with a mental change.

You have to make the mental decision to lose the weight. You have to decide how much weight you're going to lose, when you're going to lose it by, and how you're going to go about doing it. You have to make the mental voluntary decision that you will commit yourself to losing that weight no matter what.

Afterwards, you have to follow through with that voluntary decision to lose weight. You have to mentally decide what to eat, when to exercise, and how to change and adapt your lifestyle to become healthier. No one else is going to do it for you, which is why so many people struggle with weight loss. The voluntary change of the weight loss is the difficult part; the voluntary change of habits that are so familiar and ingrained, is so difficult. It's a complete mental shift in your way of thinking about food, and your relationship with it. But the change for weight loss isn't just a mental one. It's not just the voluntary decision to lose the weight. It's not just the creation of an action plan, a diet, or an exercise regimen. If it were that easy, everyone would be able to lose weight. No, weight loss touches upon so many different realms of your life. Weight loss affects nearly every aspect of you.

The capability to lose weight affects your emotions. It involves a complete modification of the way you feel about food. It involves a complete shift in the emotional responses that drive you to crave bad food in the first place. Most people turn to food in order to cure some internal strife or dilemma that they're having in their minds. The emotions begin to wreak havoc on people, forcing them to turn to food because they can't deal with those emotions. It's an emotion-numbing experience that all too many people are familiar with. If you can't deal with the emotional setbacks that are involved when you decide to lose weight, it can become nearly impossible. That's because your emotions drive you, and those emotions stem from your thoughts – thoughts you have in your conscious mind, and thoughts you have in your subconscious mind. Your body begins screaming out in resistance to all of the change, signaling a mental and emotional tumult that leaves many people crippled in its wake.

But even beyond the emotional aspect of it, weight loss affects everything else as well. It affects your spirituality. The decisions that you make in life about faith, religion, and your higher power come into play with weight loss. Some people can leverage their spirituality in the pursuit of weight loss, and other goals that involve both voluntary and involuntary change. They leverage their higher power when they need to adapt in order to thrive, and not just survive. But weight loss can tax even your spirituality. It can change how you feel emotionally on the inside by uprooting your central nervous system. These are the kinds of major changes that occur, which call everything else into question, bringing forth frustration, anxiety, and frayed nerves.

And of course, there is the physical change involved in weight loss. As you lose weight and cut down on the foods that your body was once accustomed to, it must now adapt to this physical change. The physical change in nutrients being delivered to your body, and the fat content that it receives, is severe. The physical response of your body's cells to the change can wreak havoc on most people. People have a lot of difficulty adapting to the kind of physical change created by dieting. Everything inside of you begins changing. Your entire physical makeup is uprooted. Cells that were once used to receiving so much sugar, fat, and salt, have to now adapt themselves to the new intake of food composition.

It's hard to make the kinds of drastic changes that are required for people trying to lose weight, which is why most people fail. It's hard to be able to balance the emotional, physical, mental, and spiritual demands that a goal like major weight loss has on the body. It's hard to be able to cope with the time, and preparation involved, with leading a healthy lifestyle, especially when you're so accustomed to fast, easy food. But the failure in weight loss occurs not from lacking the "want" to lose weight; it's from lacking the "must" to lose weight. The change doesn't occur here because it wasn't a "must" for the person. It wasn't a "must" and they didn't believe truly in their core that they could do it. They didn't believe that no matter what happened, what obstacles came in their way, they would tackle them, and they would persevere.

Weight loss is just one such example of change that touches the very heart of who we are and all the decisions that we make on a daily basis. And the never-ending search by some for a successful weight loss program really resides in their capability to do one thing – adapt to voluntary change. When you can adapt to voluntary change, you can do just about anything. When you have the mental, emotional, physical, and spiritual capacity, to embrace voluntary change on every level, you can accomplish any goal, overcome any obstacle, and fulfill any dream in life. When you can embody the type of embrace of voluntary change required, that takes things from being a "should," to being a "must," you truly can move mountains. You can do anything.

But where does the ability to change come from? How is it that some people are so able to quickly adapt to voluntary change, whereas others falter? How is it that it's seemingly so easy for some people to make a decision to do something, or achieve some goal, to set out and just do it? They don't wait around for some miraculous occasion, they simply make the decision, and they do it. They create voluntary change on a massive scale. How is that possible? How can some people do this so easily, and so effortlessly? With strong enough beliefs, that's how. It all boils down to a person's beliefs. If the beliefs are strong enough to support the voluntary change, then it will trump all other demands on the mental, emotional, physical, and spiritual body of a person.

ADAPTABILITY TO CHANGE

Adaptability to change plays a major role in the success of a person's goals. But this applies to both voluntary and involuntary change. Because sometimes in life, change is involuntary, and that involuntary change can either make or break a person, business, or other entity. Involuntary change can uproot a person's life, disrupt business practices, or shift behavioral patterns, to negatively affect any one person or entity. But involuntary changes happen all the time, whether it's major or minor. From stock market crashes, to recessions, to a shift in fads, and so on, involuntary change is happening all around us. We can't control all of the factors of life, so we must learn to adapt to the change as it happens. Your ability to adapt to this change, whether voluntary or involuntary, will dictate your potential for success.

When people or businesses can't adapt to change, change runs them over. We see this happen all the time. A perfect example is the income example. When a person is used to receiving a certain level of income, then that level of income dramatically changes, the person can either adapt to survive, thrive, or experience a slow financial death. If someone can't alter their expenses and spending habits when income changes like this happen, they can't survive, let alone thrive. Not only can't they survive, but also, they'll slowly whither away financially, which creates emotional havoc on their internal nervous system, thus further affecting their physical bodies, their minds, and the strength of their spirits. Everything goes into a free-fall decline.

We see this all the time, not only in individuals, but also in businesses as well. When a corporation can't adapt to the changing business environment, they can fail, and suffer a slow and painful corporate death. Eastman Kodak failed to adapt to changing demands in the marketplace, forcing it to file for bankruptcy in January of 2012. The once behemoth innovator in the industry, fell victim to the quick advancements of digital photography. Although Eastman Kodak was left with a very large and valuable collection of patents, it lost its vital core photo film and processing business revenues. If you can't adapt to change, change will run you over. But, if you can embrace it, change can go from adversary to friend very quickly.

Other companies were able to adapt to change, and in fact embrace that change by investing heavily in areas affecting their businesses that were experiencing the most change. Those companies not only survived, they were able to thrive. They were able to leverage the changing tides in the marketplace, and effectively make the internal voluntary changes necessary to respond to the external involuntary changes that were occurring. Companies like IBM, Apple, and Berkshire Hathaway are clear winners in the adaptability department. They were able to adapt, expand their vision, and position their companies for change, investing in the right areas, at the right time. They weren't just able to survive; these companies were able to thrive, all by applying consistent action to adapt to change on a daily basis.

But change isn't just something that happens to businesses or even people, change is something that happens across every single spectrum known to man. Whether it's changing seasons, bird migrations, erupting volcanoes, tectonic plates shifting, and everything in between, changes are happening all around us, all of the time. But there's something deeper, at the heart of it all, that affects your ability to adapt to change. There's something more profound at work, at the very core of who you are. It lies at the heart of businesses, countries, economies, religions, and everything else that makes the world go round – and those are beliefs. It's not just about being able to change, or want to change; it's about believing you can change. If you don't embody the belief that you can, and will, do everything necessary to adapt to change, you will never be able to. If you can't embody the relentless mindset required to adapt to change, change will run you over. You will never be able to conquer your goals, or overcome your obstacles, without the clear and utter belief that you achieve anything you put your mind to, including, adapting to change in every which way necessary.

Anytime you have a person, company, or entity that has the conscious belief that will empower them to thrive, then they will. That's because it's not just about survival. Survival is part of our instinct. Survival is basal to us. We survive without thinking about it. When it comes to financial survival, people will usually do whatever it takes to stay afloat. While some do too little to late, eventually, they must be able to adapt to the involuntary changing tides in their lives, or suffer the drastic consequences of their actions. They don't have much of a choice. Whether it's a business or a person, they will usually do what it takes to survive, because that's just programmed within us.

The survival instinct is an important one to highlight. It's important to look at our necessity for survival. When something is a "must," we do whatever it takes to survive, but when something is a "should," we don't seem to put forth the same amount of effort. Why do you think that is? Why do you think that when we have to do something, we seem to be able to step up to the plate and get things done? A perfect example of this is with television game shows that deal with having to complete a certain task, within a certain amount of time. These competitive game shows force people to have to be done on time, in order to win a certain prize. They have to finish, and the final product has to look good, in order to win the prize.

While a game show isn't a basal survival instinct, the people on the shows do seem to be done just in the right amount of time. The brain is somehow able to know just what actions it needs to perform, and just how quickly it needs to perform them, in order to finish and win. It's something that goes on behind the scenes that people aren't even aware of. It happens in the subconscious mind. The amount of processing, analyzing, and deconstructing done by the mind, is phenomenal. But the mind will only do so much for you. It has to be motivated to act, and that motivation comes from within. That motivation comes from an ingrained set of beliefs that are akin to the person used to setting goals and achieving them.

What's also important to understand here is the pleasure and pain paradigm. Human beings will always do more to avoid pain, than they will to gain pleasure. So, if your mind knows about a specific deadline, and if you don't meet that deadline, it's going to mean a lot of pain, it will do whatever it takes in order to make you meet that deadline so that it doesn't experience the pain. It's doing more to avoid pain than gain pleasure. An example of this would be the filing of taxes on time; dealing with dental problems that eventually worsen to the point where you have to see the dentist; or, dealing with major health scares, usually after something major has happened such as a heart attack or a stroke.

THE ORIGIN OF BELIEFS

Beliefs are powerful. They are at the core of who you are, and at the very heart of why it is you do what you do. Imagine for a moment what your own beliefs impact in your life. How do your beliefs shape and sculpt the many different areas of how you live your life? From your religion, to your relationships, to your decisions about politics, to how you spend your money, to what foods you eat, to how you feel about the environment, and everything in between – all the decisions that you make in life are affected by your beliefs. If you believe that, "Money is the root of all evil," you'll certainly operate your finances differently from someone who believes that, "Money can buy happiness." If you believe that all people are liars and cheats, you will have a very different view on politics, than someone who trusts in people wholeheartedly.

So, if beliefs affect the decisions in your life, it's safe to say that if you want to make massive changes in your life, you have to have the right, empowering beliefs. You also have to understand why you believe the things that you do first, before you can make any major strides towards changing those beliefs, and your life, for the better. Without first understanding what you believe in, making major change, and subsequently major progress, would be next to impossible. That's because, you could set yourself up for a situation where your goals and your beliefs are disharmonious. In essence, that would mean that you might not actually want the things that you think you want, badly enough. Because, when you do want something badly enough, and you believe strongly enough, in your core, that you will accomplish that goal, nothing can stand in your way. That's when you can move mountains. But it starts with your underlying beliefs. Without the right empowering beliefs, you can't support the voluntary changes you're after.

But understanding your beliefs is easier said than done. Understanding why you do the things you do, isn't very simple. That's because, oftentimes we're walking dichotomies, contradicting ourselves, or criticizing others for the same things, we've done ourselves in the past. This calls our beliefs into question. If we think we feel really strongly about something, why do we criticize others when we've done the same things in the past? We become critical beings that shroud our own insecurities by highlighting those of others. We're all guilty of doing this, but it's usually not by choice. This behavior is part of the psychic apparatus that's built into our psyches, which develops from a very early age. This also acts as a defense mechanism, created by the ego, to shroud some of our inner fears and anxieties. We tend to call others out on things that we ourselves are insecure about.

Anytime you're pursuing a goal that you eventually give up on, it's because you didn't possess the underlying belief that was strong enough, or congruent enough with you, to see it through. You didn't have the foundational underlying beliefs, in order to persevere. You may have thought that you did at one point, but when it came down to it, you buckled and cracked. I can't tell you how many times this has happened to me in the past. I can recall many situations where I thought I really wanted something, worked hard initially towards it, then hit a wall, or simply got too comfortable. Oftentimes, after a small bit of initial success, I would begin to ease back into old repetitive patterns of behavior that only worked to self serve my ego. But at the time, when it was happening, I couldn't see any problem with my own behavior. My ego was so good at shrouding my behavior, that it was completely hidden from me on a conscious level. Everyone else was wrong, except for me, all the time. Does this sound familiar?

My ego had been so busy creating its own set of beliefs that only helped to seemingly shroud me from any emotional pain or suffering that I may have experienced, that I actually had developed two sets of beliefs. What most people don't realize is that, they too have two sets of beliefs as well. They have one set of beliefs created by their ego, which runs the negative thought patterns through their minds. And, another set of beliefs that are consciously created in the hopes to help support our pursuits in life. Examples of the ego's beliefs may be statements like, "I'm just big boned," for someone trying to lose weight, that can't; "You need money to make money," for someone who may have failed to get a business off the ground; or, "I don't really have a drinking problem," for an alcoholic who falls off the wagon. You see the ego was busy creating all of these negative beliefs – or excuses if you may – so that it could protect you at that point when you needed it most. The ego's beliefs actually supersede the conscious beliefs we think we have, that try to support our goals. When you decided to give up, ego's beliefs acted as the crutches that helped to hold and support you when you faltered.

Beliefs can be powerful, whether they help to support you, or hurt you. What you have to understand is that, the beliefs that help to hurt you, and don't support you, are only there thanks to the ego. And abolishing those negative beliefs isn't impossible, but it does take a significant amount of honesty and awareness on your part. No matter what you want, you can see that through in life. If you don't believe strongly enough in something at your core, then giving up is easy. Even in the face of failure, people who have developed strong enough beliefs, always succeed. It's the hallmark of success. It's important to work to understand your own core underlying beliefs, if you want to make massive changes in your life – if you want to move mountains.

You can also leverage the pleasure and pain paradigm to help fuel your pursuit of goals in life. You can use the fact that you will do more to avoid pain, than you will to gain pleasure. You can do this with careful self-analysis, and a shift in the paradigm through a way of thinking. For example, most people that smoke cigarettes know that it's bad for them. Most people are conscious of the negative effects that cigarette smoking has on their bodies. This is something that is very clear today, and much more so than it ever was. However, many people still smoke cigarettes. Even with knowing that a cigarette is bad for them, people continue to engage in smoking them. Why do you think that is?

With cigarette smoking, you've attributed more pain to quitting, than the pleasure of continuing to smoke. That's because cigarette smoking is a habit, and a behavior, that brings short-term pleasure. It's an immediate escape, or a tool that people use to calm their nerves. But everyone knows that cigarette smoking is doing more long-term damage to him or her than the short-term pleasure they're receiving. But although they may know that, they continue to smoke. That's because the mind's pleasure and pain paradigm is setup for short-term gratification. Since you don't see the long-term negative effects of cigarette smoking for years, most people are easily able to avoid thinking about them. These people may know that cigarette smoking is bad for them in the long-term, but their minds block that out in order to receive the instant gratification of smoking in the short-term.

In order to flip the pleasure and pain paradigm of pleasure in the short-term, with pain in the short-term, you'll need to understand more about these types of urges and how they're developed in the mind. I'll be covering this in the coming chapter, but a careful analysis of the long-term effects of cigarette smoking can help you quit, but you must associate enough pain with the cigarette smoking in the long-term, in order to do so. But most people aren't capable of doing this. They're unable to look at the long-term negative effects. But after a while, it becomes harder and harder to do this as well. That's because not only has the mind built an instant pleasure habit to smoking, it's also evolved into a behavior that's not easily replaceable. It's not easily replaceable because it's become ingrained in you. It's become your go to tool for stress-reduction and relaxation.

This type of short-term instant gratification and pleasure applies to everything else in life as well. For example, most people associate the short-term pleasure that they'll gain by eating a fast food meal, to be far more beneficial to them than the long-term negative effects it will have. Again, like the cigarette smoking, the eating of junk food and unhealthy meals becomes a habit and a behavior that becomes ingrained. But unlike cigarette smoking, eating bad food is not a physical addiction. The physical addiction of smoking cigarettes makes it even harder to quit. However, the habit of eating unhealthy foods, that offer a quick burst of sugar and carbohydrates, is a mental addiction. Although the body develops a physical "craving" for that type of food, the pleasure in the short-term is more associated to the mind. This makes the habit of eating junk food very difficult to break.

Anytime you get accustomed to a particular behavior, habit or pattern, it becomes difficult to break. Anytime you look to the short-term pleasurable benefits as opposed to the long-term pain it may cause, you'll continue to revert to the former. If you can't associate enough pain to the long-term activity, then you won't be able to make the changes that are required. It's incredibly difficult to do so, especially when the change is a voluntary one. For example, most people are much more likely to change their habits, when they become life threatening. From the cigarette smoker's lung cancer scare, to the drug abusers overdose, to the overly obese person's heart attack, as soon as the short-term pain begins to outweigh the short-term pleasure, people have a tendency to adapt and change at a much higher rate. But that's also because it shifts from a voluntary change to more of an involuntary change – they must adapt in order to survive.

But why does it take some calamity or strife to change behavior that we all know is detrimental to us? Why does it take something like a heart attack to begin losing weight? Why does it take the scare of lung cancer to stop smoking cigarettes? And, why do habitual drug users need multiple overdose scares to get them to quit? Again, this comes back to the pleasure and pain paradigm, but it's more than just that. It's a conditioning and a set of beliefs that have been created and ingrained in your subconscious mind that are difficult to change. Once a belief has been set, it's very difficult to get someone's mind to alter that belief. That's because of the subconscious self-talk that goes on in the mind that you're unaware of. Beliefs also strengthen over time – the ego will search out and find more supporting experiences for that particular belief, to sustain its attempts to protect your fragile inner self. But once you believe that the short-term pleasure will in fact be short-term pain, you can begin on the road to altering your behavior to help support you, and not hinder you.

3

UNDERSTANDING THE EGO

"One may understand the cosmos, but never the ego; the self is more distant than any star." – Gilbert Chesterton

Patrick woke up to the incessant sound of his alarm clock. It was Monday morning – another start to the workweek. The 29-year-old bachelor lived in the outskirts of Miami's South Beach and had to commute to work past glitzy yachts and multi-million dollar mansions every single day. It was as though they were all taunting him. He didn't want to wake up. Just the thought of having to go back into that office gave him the chills. He was tired of it. He was tired of how he felt cold calling people, trying to sell them products and services they had absolutely no use for. He hated how he felt when the fluorescent white tubes of death, shining light from above, sucked the energy right out of him. He hated all of it.

But Patrick had no choice. He had to work. The barely-above minimum wage job, plus commissions, was his only bread and butter. It was his fourth job in as many years, and he couldn't seem to hold it together long enough at one company to make any major strides. He wasn't sure what to do anymore, but he had no choice. He had an oversized car loan he had to pay for, rent he was barely getting by with, and he had to have money to eat and go out with his friends with. What else would there be if all he did were work? How boring would life become? Patrick didn't want to even continue down that thought pattern. He had to keep things going. He had to keep it together.

The alarm clock rang again. He must have dozed off. "Shoot!" He yelled. "I'm gonna be late again." In fact, Patrick was usually late, and that morning would be no different. Although he had promised himself he wouldn't be going out with his friends until he could save up some more money, the night before, when he received a text from his friends who were all out on the town, he couldn't resist. With only three hours of sleep, and a raging hangover, Patrick was a wreck from the night before. He quickly jumped in the shower, shaved, and got ready for work. He could barely think straight. "How am I going to give this sales presentation?"

Heat. Traffic. Noise. His head was pounding. The commute to work was awful. He felt like puking the entire way in. He felt even more disgusted as he passed over the bridge to look off at Star Island and see the glitzy mansions and yachts once again. "Ugh, how am I ever going to get that?" He was a mess, and nearly an hour late through the door of the office, Patrick was out of breath. "I should really quit smoking cigarettes," he thought to himself. But Patrick's life was all but falling apart. He was barely keeping it together.

As he sat down in his office chair and placed his headset on his head, his phone buzzed. "Patrick, get in here." It was his boss. He knew it was only a matter of time before they had "that chat" again. He was dreading it, and to make matters worse, he looked like he had been to hell and back.

"You wanted to speak to me, sir?" Patrick ran his hand through his disheveled hair that flopped back in front of his face again, as he timidly hovered near the entry to his boss's office. He was unkempt and sluggish, and it showed.

"Yes, sit down."

"Sir, I'm really sorry. I... I know what you're going to say but..."

"Actually, don't sit down. You're fired. Pack up your things and leave." Patrick's boss was through with him. It was the umpteenth time he was late to work and he wasn't producing any results. He had to let him go.

"But... but sir, you can't. Please. I have rent to pay. This is the worst possible time. Please."

"Are you serious? I'm running a business here, kid, not a daycare. If you had cared about your job, you would have listened to me the last time we had this same conversation. I can't even remember how many times this has been."

"Please. Sir. I really need this. I really need this job. I promise from here on out that I'll never be late again. Please. Don't do this." The fact of the matter was that he really needed the job, but he hated the job. He had mixed feelings about it, and it showed in his performance. He didn't really want the job; he wanted the menial pay from the job that let him just barely skirt by and survive.

"Nope. That's it kid. You're done."

Patrick grabbed a very small box and gathered the few belongings he had at the office. He looked around, and felt sorry for them. No, he felt sorry for himself. Or, did he feel sorry for them? He wasn't quite sure; he felt mixed feelings about being fired. He couldn't understand why he had gone out the night before, when he knew he had to be in for work and give a sales presentation early the next day. Plus, he still had a severe hangover, and he wasn't quite sure why he decided to drive into work. He was still probably drunk from the night before. He just wasn't quite sure what was wrong with him.

"What am I going to do now?" he thought to himself. "I need to figure this out. I need to find a new job, and fast." Those thoughts kept running through his mind. He had switched into survival mode. He wasn't sure why he kept behaving this way. He wasn't quite sure why he kept self-sabotaging himself every chance he got. He never used to be like this. What went wrong? He didn't understand why he couldn't control his own behavior. He didn't understand why he was making such poor decisions in life. He just didn't understand.

*****

Many people are familiar with their egos, but many people aren't truly familiar with how their egos work. Many people don't understand just how the mental self-talk that goes on in your mind evolves, and where it comes from. They're not aware of the power of thought, and how negative thought seedlings sowed in the mind, could reap negative results in reality. Some people are slaves to this mental battle that goes on in their minds. The ego imprisons them, manipulating and altering their thoughts patterns for its own self-preservation.

People do really become slaves to their minds and their egos. On the one hand, they think they want something, but on the other hand, they realize that maybe they don't really want it that bad. They realize they don't want it that bad by their own actions. They find themselves planning and wanting to attain or achieve certain things, but when it comes time to achieve them, they end up reverting to old negative patterns and behaviors. But it doesn't have to be that way. You don't have to be a slave to your own ego. You don't have to be a pawn in the chess game going on in your mind. You can control your ego, to an extent, but before you can even fathom doing that, you must understand more about your ego and just how it works.

The ego is important because it's critical to you, and why you do the things that you do. Without a firm understanding of your ego, and how your mind works, you can't truly begin to deconstruct your behavior, and see where it is you've been going wrong. You can't accomplish any real goals, let alone move mountains that may stand in the way of your goals. But by understanding the ego, you can begin to decompile the instructional statements that are constantly being entered into the computer that's your mind. But imagine not being able to read and write in a certain software language, and trying to debug a program in that language. It would be next to impossible. You have to understand how the software program works first, and the programming language itself, in order to be able to make any modifications or upgrades.

The mind is very similar to a computer in that way. It has tiny little parts that are all working in conjunction with one another. Your mind, or the CPU of your brain, is at the heart of all that you are and do. It controls all of your body's functions, thoughts, processes, analyses, and decisions, both subconsciously, and consciously. But the ego is a very complex thing, and it's often difficult for us to diagnose our own problems, since the ego does such a good job of hiding and shrouding our own shortcomings in its protective layer. For example, say you have a friend that you know is doing something detrimental to their health, or well-being. Maybe they're living a certain lifestyle that's hurting them in one way or another, they have some addiction, or they're in a toxic relationship, but they're unable to acknowledge it. They're unable to admit that they have a problem because their ego gets in the way. The ego gets in the way, because it's designed not to find flaws in itself. That wouldn't serve its needs for survival. The ego wants to survive, and your being and all that you do cannot be called into question by your ego – until something major goes wrong in your life – so the ego will help you find reasons why it supports your behavior. But we shouldn't have to wait until we hit those rock bottoms in life to uncover our shortcomings.

But what is the ego really and how does it work? Well, ego is the Latin word for "I," or the self, of any one person, and it's very much a part of you. It's just as much a part of you as are the limbs attached to your body. It's as much a part of you as your true inner self is. But, let's face it, the ego is really the protective shell, or film, that's wrapped around that fragile inner self. It's been designed to protect your inner self from things like hurt, rejection, pain, and other negative emotions. The ego is merely a projection of the inner self, based on a person's experiences and beliefs. It's there to help protect that fragile inner part of you that's so easily hurt and so accustomed to emotion-numbing behaviors. It's there to act as a built-in support system to see you through the failures and rejections in life.

In fact, the ego is part of a complex series of components in your mind called the psychic apparatus. The psychic apparatus is a term coined by the late and notable psychiatrist, Sigmund Freud, who spent his life's work on developing an understanding of our internal psychology. The physic apparatus is merely a product – or a projection – of the mind and is not part of the physical brain in our bodies. However, the psychic apparatus is the driver of the car that is your brain, so it very much controls the way in which you live your life, and the decisions that you make – it's the embedded and learned software program that runs the mind. The psychic apparatus dictates your decisions, your lifestyle, and helps you form the beliefs that you harbor.

Genetically speaking, we are embedded with a certain number of natural drives and impulses. We are creatures of survival and pleasure, and it's in our instinct to do things like eat, sleep, and procreate. But as babies, we have only one component of the three-part psychic apparatus that exists in adults. That component is called the *id*. The id is the part of the psychic apparatus that is instinctive, and genetically installed, or pre-conditioned in us. It's what gives us those urges to eat, sleep, and procreate. It's where our sexual libido and tendencies towards aggression stems from, and the id is merely there to seek instant gratification. This part of the personality also operates on the pleasure principle. It simply seeks to gain pleasure or gratification without consequence. The id doesn't know right from wrong, or good from bad. It is instinctual, native, and pre-existing. If your psychic apparatus were left only up to your id, there would be nothing stopping you from doing what you wanted at any given moment in time. You may walk into a restaurant, not want to wait, and begin snatching food off tables. You might walk into a store and take what you like, or even say what you like to anyone around you at any time without consequence. It's a good thing we're not only controlled by the id.

At the other far end of the spectrum of the psychic apparatus, is the super-ego. The super-ego is the part of you that's developed through the moral guidance of your parents or guardians, along with the morals that you develop within your culture, your society, and your religion. The super-ego helps to play the more critical role in your life, and help you to understand the good from the bad. It acts as the yang to the yin of the id. And in between these two components, is the ego itself. The ego, or the "I," is the part of the psychic apparatus that operates under the reality principle. It's also part of the id, which is developed through experiential knowledge of the world. As you grow and mature, a part of the id breaks off and forms into the ego and the super-ego. The ego uses more reason and rational to its actions, and it works to balance the yin and the yang of the id and the super-ego. It acts as the go between. The ego is what allows you to co-exist with other people, and it bases its decisions on the reality principle. It seeks to help you get the pleasure of the id, in realistic ways that will benefit over the longer term. However, the ego is constantly trying to please itself and the other parts of the psychic apparatus, creating a constant struggle for dominance in the mind.

The resultant interaction between the id, the ego, and the super-ego, lead you to create certain beliefs in your life. As you grow and mature, your id has certain urges, which are counter-balanced by the moral scruples of the super-ego. But it's the ego, which acts as the referee of the mind, helping to decide which decisions you ultimately make. When the balance is skewed towards the id, you might do things that you later regret, or feel guilty about. The super-ego is what creates guilt, or resentment, when this occurs. The super-ego is there to act as the pain, in the pleasure and pain paradigm. The pleasure and pain paradigm of course states that you'll do more to avoid pain than you will to gain pleasure. So, in example, most people in the United States file their taxes the day before they're due on April 15th of the year. They generally wait until the last minute to finally get to it just before it's due at midnight on the 15th of April. That's because they have now gone into a mode where they realize that the pain of not filing their taxes is going to far exceed the pleasure of putting it off any longer. This is where the super-ego begins weighing heavily on the mind, and the ego's refereeing tilts your decision to act towards the super-ego, as opposed to the id. This same rule applies with many other things in life such as, students cramming for exams or writing papers the day or night before, people going on crash diets, and so on.

Another layer of complexity to the psychic apparatus is the conscious and subconscious process of the three different components. The id is a purely subconscious component, existing only in the basal and instinctive urges for pleasure. We don't make decisions about the id; it makes its own decisions. At times, those decisions can be temptations, or urges that compel individuals to do things that they may later regret, such as cheat on their spouses, or commit crimes. However, the ego, and the super-ego, reside both in the conscious, and subconscious realms. The varying degree of subconscious, and conscious processes, help to also weigh just how many people make their decisions.

If a person is consciously aware of the ego, and super-ego interactions, then their decisions may posses more moral scruple. People that are less aware of these processes are more likely to succumb to the emotion-numbing behavior of the ego, because although the ego is rooted in reality, when you lack awareness of the ego and super-ego's interactions, you are merely a slave to its decisions. And, the ego will generally default to the id's pleasure principle when it can't see the short-term negative effects of the emotion-numbing activities it reverts you to. This applies to any decision or behavior that involves a significant amount of voluntary change from present behavior. Things like weight loss, good grades, saving money, fidelity, and so on, are all affected by this interaction. The ego will always try to take you back to your old habits and patterns, to save you the feelings of humiliation, fear, and upset that come with potentially failing.

When you begin to recognize that no success is possible without failure, and you become more acutely aware of the self-talk of your ego and super-ego in your mind, you can accomplish anything. No matter what's thrown your way, you will overcome it because you begin to realize, and build an awareness, of what this interaction is that's taking place in your mind. Then, you're no longer a slave to its decisions, and you get to make the decisions in a conscious state. But as you may already know, we oftentimes do things that we later regret, all because we allow the subconscious mind to take over. It takes over, reverting us to our old patterns and behaviors. This is why change becomes increasingly difficult, as you grow older. This is why criminals are less likely to rehabilitate after a "career of crime." This is why it's so difficult for people who live paycheck-to-paycheck, to start saving money. It's all in the conditioning, which is hard to break unless you learn the specific skillset on how to do so. But even then, it's not that simple. It takes consistent effort, on a consistent basis, of always being conscious and aware.

If any of this sounds familiar, you're not alone of course. Whether you've been trying to lose weight, make more money, or accomplish any other goal, you know by now it's not simple. You know by now that, although you may set out to write out the goals for what you want in life, when push comes to shove, the id usually wins. It's that little voice in your mind driving you, and pushing you to just revert to your old habits. It's that little voice in your mind that says, "It's okay, go ahead, just one candy bar won't hurt," or "You can save next month, one day of shopping won't kill you." This goes against all of your cognitive reasoning, and most people usually just succumb to their "weak will," as most would put it. These are the excuses, or negative belief systems, that are installed by the ego. They are so covertly hidden from the conscious mind, that unless you work to uncover these negative beliefs, and truly eradicate them, you'll be faced with the same patterns of behavior the next time you set out to accomplish something.

THE INSTALLATION OF BELIEFS

As we grow and are raised, our ego plays a major role in molding and shaping our beliefs. Those beliefs are essentially fundamental choices that you've made about how the world works. Some of those beliefs are truths – which would include things like gravity, and other laws that would be based on physics and mathematics – and others are just beliefs on the way you think the world works. Your ego and super-ego worked to shape the beliefs that you have today through experiential knowledge. This means that as you grew up, and had certain experiences, your outcome from those experiences helped you to form your beliefs.

One example of a belief would be the statement "I am beautiful, and people love me." In order to form that belief, you had to have had experiences in your life that led you to believe that you are beautiful, and that people do in fact love you. Of course, your definition of beauty and love here will play a large role in forming this belief, but at the end of the day, your belief is just that – it's a belief. If you believe that you are beautiful and that people love you, then you most likely go about your life much differently than someone who believes, "I am ugly and nobody likes me." Each of these people will operate their lives in a considerably different way, with different expectations, due to this one core belief.

However, it's also the case that you encounter many people who seem to possess the most unlikely traits, and harbor very unlikely beliefs. Have you ever met a man or woman who was say average or below-average looking, but they acted in a way that conveyed their confidence in their looks? Even though they may not seem to be that good looking, something about the way they behave conveys beauty. Not through arrogance, but through a true belief that they are beautiful or handsome, some people are able to impress that upon others. Somewhere along the line, they developed the core belief that they are beautiful. All of their experiences led them to believe, deep down inside, that they are truly beautiful or handsome. They developed an empowering core belief.

When we talk about core beliefs, I'm really referring to a belief that is almost like a truth to you. When you have a core belief, you hold that almost as true as you would something based in physics. If you were to say, "All politicians are liars," you might hold that as a truth, meaning that, no amount of reasoning will allow you to be convinced otherwise. I wouldn't be able to sway you from your belief about politicians. Of course, a belief like this would also make you operate your life, and behave, in a much different way than a person who believes otherwise. If you were to tell the very secure person, who has developed the core belief that they are beautiful, that they in fact are ugly, they would most likely laugh it off. That's because it's a core belief. It's not a belief created by the ego, but rather, one created by the inner self that's harbored as the complete and utter truth.

Can you see just how important beliefs are here? The problem is that you have this set of beliefs that have been developed and installed throughout your childhood and adult life, and they now affect everything from how you see money, to food, to relationships, and everything in between. But it's only really a problem when they are beliefs that are limiting beliefs, and not empowering ones. When people develop empowering beliefs, they can seemingly conquer and achieve just about anything they set their minds to. That's because, when you believe in something so wholeheartedly like that, nothing can sway your mind. Nothing can come between you and your belief of how you see the world, or your true inner self, when it's a core inner belief. But the problem is that most of us possess limiting beliefs that don't empower us.

In the past, if you've tried to achieve some goal or overcome some obstacle, and you were unable to do it, it was because of your beliefs. You didn't believe strongly enough in yourself, and in the outcome of your goals. You didn't have a strong enough reason as to why you had to achieve your goals, and you didn't believe wholeheartedly that you could. When this happens, you allow the ego to succumb to the id, and the old pleasurable patterns and behaviors kick in, rather than continuing to sit through and struggle with overcoming some obstacle. When you don't wholeheartedly believe in yourself, and you don't create that support system of very strong beliefs, you're bound to give up. You're bound to succumb to the pleasures of life that are at your beck and call wherever you may turn.

This psychic apparatus is a powerful thing. As you can see, you have three different components of your mind, all vying for your attention. From pleasure, to realism, to pain, they all want your attention. They all want to make you feel comfortable within your own skin, so they will all create very compelling reasons as to why you should choose one way or the other. The problem is that most of this happens in your mind without your awareness. You don't have control over the subconscious mechanisms in the psychic apparatus, unless you learn to control the conscious aspects of it. And even then, it's difficult to supersede the subconscious programming that's been implanted in your mind, unless you recondition it and replace the limiting beliefs with empower ones. You don't know why you're doing the things that you do until you learn to see the error of your ways. But without full, complete awareness, and honesty, your mind will trample all over you in ways that will limit and stifle your future potential.

In the past, if you gave up on a diet, a relationship, a business, or anything else in life, it's because you didn't strong enough beliefs to support your goals, in the first place. If you believed strongly enough in it, or in your ability to overcome any obstacle, you would have persevered. You see, total failure only happens when we completely give up and stop trying. When you allow the ego to take over, then you simply become a slave to your basal instincts. You may rather kick back on your couch and watch television, than say work on a supplementary income idea in the evening. Your determination and drive come from your beliefs. You have to believe strongly enough in order to succeed.

The problem is that your beliefs are so ingrained in you that the older you get, the more difficult they are to change. Your ego becomes increasingly powerful as the years go by, especially if it usually wins by allowing you to succumb to the temptations of the id. Every single time that you throw your hands up in silent resignation, or allow yourself to get sucked into the short-term pleasure trap, you allow the ego to get stronger and stronger. It provides excuses for you each time this happens, allowing you to revert to your emotion-numbing behaviors and patterns. It must do this in a sort of self-preservation manner, because it's protecting that fragile part of you that's so easily hurt and upset – it's protecting your inner self. So, even if you think you might want something in your pursuit of a goal or dream, you may be outnumbered by your ego's desires to help protect you from potential failure, or any emotional fallout that may come in the face of adversity.

4

BEHAVIORAL ANALYSIS

"Human behavior flows from three sources: desire, emotion, and knowledge. — Plato

Holden opened the restaurant door for his date, as he followed the fair-skinned blonde-haired girl, with a wide-eyed smile, into the Italian eatery. It was the second time they were having dinner in as many days, and he was excited, to say the least. After they were seated in the far corner of the dimly-lit room, he couldn't help but keep his eyes off her. She was a striking beauty, and she was there with him – all his. It didn't feel real. "So, what are you in the mood for?" he asked.

"Oh, everything. I'm starving," she said, her hazel-green eyes sparkling in the glowing ember of the tiny candelabra at the center of the intimate table. "But, I like little plates. So maybe we can share a few things?" She smiled again at him. He melted when she smiled at him.

He couldn't get that smile out of his head. The last night he spent in bed after dropping her off, was torture for him. He could barely get any sleep in the excitement to see her the next day. When he did finally manage to fall asleep, she was all he could dream about. It almost didn't feel real to him. He knew he really liked the girl, but there was something conflicting him in the back of his mind.

"Sure, we can share a few things. I love this restaurant. I used to come here all the time with... err, last year it was my favorite place to eat." He had to catch himself before talking about his on-again off-again ex-girlfriend. He knew it was too soon to talk about that. But as the thought entered his mind, he began thinking about her.

The waiter walked over and took the couple's order, but gave Holden a strange glance. He was polite, but Holden could read his mind. He had seen him there before. In fact, it was only last week that he came to that restaurant with his, "soon to be" ex-girlfriend. Yes, he had to admit it to himself – he hadn't actually completely broken it off with her yet. And he wasn't quite sure what he was waiting for. He liked the stability of being in a relationship with her, but it lacked any of the excitement he was after. Sometimes, he felt like he was at odds with himself. It was almost as if there was this infighting going on in his mind. He couldn't quite explain it, but when he looked over at the pretty girl in front of him, she just made him so happy. But then, his soon to be ex-girlfriend still made him happy at times. He wasn't quite sure if the grass was actually greener on the other side. Maybe that's why he was still holding out.

Holden wasn't always like this. He used to be concrete in his will, and knew what he wanted. Somewhere along the line though, things got misaligned. It's as though something came undone, and he wasn't quite sure what it was, or how to rationalize it. He feared having the conversation with a psychiatrist who might think he had split personality disorder or something. But he didn't think it was that. He just thought it was something inside of him – some desire or urge – that kept gnawing away at him. If ever there was a person who had a devil and an angel on his shoulders, it was Holden. But what was he supposed to do? How was he supposed to act in such a situation? He knew he had to break it off with one of them, but he just couldn't decide. He really couldn't decide.

"This is a really nice place," she said, her eyes sparkling again across the small table. Holden edged a smile, but she could sense something was amiss. "What's wrong? Is everything okay?"

"Yeah, it's just… oh, nothing. I mean…"

"What? What is it? Tell me. Now you've got me curious."

"I'm just happy to be here that's all." He tried to sound as convincing as possible, but he wasn't sure if she was entirely buying it.

"Are you sure there's nothing else?" She had been in similar situations before. She could almost sense what that hesitation was, but she decided to leave it for another conversation, on another day. If it even went that far, she thought to herself.

"I guess… Sometimes I just feel… conflicted. Do you know what I mean? Has that ever happened to you before?" He searched her eyes for some kind of understanding – some kind of look that would convey that she understood what he was trying to get across to her. "I just feel like I have these different voices in my head sometimes. Well, not really voices. I mean, I'm not crazy or anything. I just think that sometimes I don't know what

I want in life. Know what I mean?" He was getting deep into conversation for only the second date, and he was hoping he wouldn't scare her off.

"You know what? I know exactly what you mean. I think that at our age, sometimes, we're just really looking for that perfect situation, and we feel pushed and pulled in both directions." She knew exactly what he was talking about, but she wouldn't concede to it just yet. "I feel like that all the time, but I think it's kind of normal. We all have these different urges inside of our heads trying to get us to act one way or another. No... I know exactly what you're talking about."

Holden felt a sense of relief – still perplexed, but kind of relieved. "Yeah, I guess I feel like that. I kind of never really know. There's been so much disappointment and upset in my life that, sometimes I'm not really sure what I even want myself." He looked at her as the words came out of his mouth. He was sure she knew what he was talking about without being entirely direct about it. But before they could continue the conversation any further, the appetizers were dropped in front of them, and they were both starving.

"Wow, this looks amazing." She smiled, her eyes sparkling again, and nothing else really seemed to really matter at that point in time. "Let's eat."

*****

All too often, we fall victim to the somewhat Neanderthal like infighting taking place within our psychic apparatus. We think we want something, but we act in a contradictory manner. Has this ever happened to you?

This comes back to the whole grass is greener on the other side conversation, but how much of this is true? Are we actually never satisfied with what we have in life? Or, is it that the id-mind is constantly seeking more, and more pleasurable experiences, only to be subdued by the super-ego on occasion? So, does it mean that we always want pleasure, but have to control our urges with the super-ego? These are all interesting questions, and the level of control that exists within your mind is governed by the super-ego. That super-ego is unique to each individual, because no two people have the same exact experiences in life. Even identical twins can grow up to possess different personalities, due to the varying development of their psychic apparatuses.

But it's important to work to understand your own mind, and your own behavior, so that you don't become a slave to the infighting going on in it. In the pursuit of any goal, hope, or dream, an underlying understanding of your behavior is critical to those pursuits, because your behavior, and actions, are at the heart of what brings those things into fruition. If you can understand and modify your behavior to serve you rather than defeat you, then you can progress towards your goals at a much more rapid rate. In another words, you won't be able to move mountains unless you can first control what's in your mind. And the study of psychology helps to uncover why we behave the way that we do. It helps to uncover the seemingly complex set of thoughts and actions, which seem to spring to life from us on its own. Yet, although we may seem complex, when for example we say and do two different things, we're actually relatively simple at the core. We're simple in the fact that, the mechanisms in our mind are straightforward and easy to understand. The complexities lie in our inability to have a personal awareness for the inner self-talk. It's hard to be that impartial third-party on the outside looking into your own mind – very hard.

At times, our own behavior can frustrate even us. When we act contrary to how we thought we felt at one point in time, it can be emotionally overwhelming. Sometimes, we can't get to the root of the problem because it's masked by so much subconscious thoughts manifested into behavior – behavior that's masked cleverly by the ego. But to uncover your own subconscious thoughts, you have to be able to be that impartial third person looking in at the self-talk in your mind. You have to be able to take an honest look at what your mind is trying to tell you. When you can build this type of honest awareness, you can uncover the inner workings of your mind, and inner desires. Sometimes, those inner desires are going to conflict with your current goals, hopes and dreams. Without bringing the inner desires – the desires of the subconscious mind – in sync with your outer conscious desires, you will find yourself at odds with yourself.

Toxicology can help to further cloud your inner desires as well, masking them from you to an even further extent. Anytime you engage in toxic behavior by indulging excessively in drugs, alcohol, cigarettes, and unclean foods, you're actually changing the neurochemical makeup in your brain. That neurochemical makeup is the same substance that your thoughts – the neurotransmissions in your mind – have to travel through. By clouding your mind with toxins, you are further deepening the disparity between the id, and the super-ego, further widening that disparity. You become more at odds with yourself, the more you cloud yourself with toxins, because your mind has difficulty seeing clearly, when this is occurring. It has difficulty with its own reasoning, and your subconscious desires begin to grow stronger, and you act out in sudden urges that normally wouldn't surface at other times. By keeping your mind and body clean and clear of toxins, you can progress towards your goals, your hopes, and your dreams without so much resistance — you can move mountains.

THE ORIGIN OF OUR BEHAVIOR

It's typically conceded that modern psychology began in the late 19th century through the careful analysis, and study in the field, by notable psychologists William James, and of course, Sigmund Freud, who some consider to be the father of modern psychology. The biggest issue that's plagued psychology for the past century has been the human struggle that exists as a result of the three components of the ego – the psychic apparatus – vying for dominance: the id, the ego, and the super-ego. On the one end of the spectrum, you have the selfish need for survival and pleasure of the id, then the practical and reality-rooted component of the ego, which allows us to co-exist with one another by balancing the id with the super-ego, the socially conscious and moral component.

The struggle that exists between the three components creates feelings of anxiety, nervousness, and worry. This happens when the components clash with one another.

The resultant behavior, or how we treat each other, along with how we treat ourselves, is ultimately determined by which one of these three forces reigns supreme. We see the most dramatic examples of this in children as they develop from babies, to toddlers, and into teenagers. The developmental psychology of their minds begins to transform and mature as they age, forming the adult mind's psychic apparatus. As toddlers and children, we are mostly a product of the id – we usually want something, and we want it now. Children don't really understand, or grasp the concept of "no," at very early ages. If they want something, they voice their opinions with no filter. They are id-creatures, to say the least. But as children grow up and mature, they learn to co-exist with other children and adults. This is where the formation of their egos and super-egos begins. But the id is the most prevalent force at work for children. It's usually not until their later years that they begin to develop a moral compass and implant both an ego and super-ego. This creates an enormous amount of anxiety for children as they begin to learn the rules of their new worlds, and develop their minds to try to adapt to life within society and its rules.

So, your behavior then is a direct product of these three forces working within you. But these forces are founded upon their own experiential knowledge and development. Meaning, that if you've been through positive experiences, and developed positive beliefs due to those experiences, the resultant, or dominant force, will be different than someone who has had many negative experiences, and developed negative beliefs. The ego and super-ego will develop differently than someone who has had far different experiences. This is true no matter what area of life we talk about.

For example, if you've tried to lose weight in the past and you've had negative experiences, you've developed some negative beliefs that now live both in your subconscious, and conscious mind. You can't see the ones buried in the subconscious mind, because those are stored there as self-preservation, or defense mechanisms, by the ego. And those beliefs stored through experiences are what will control your dominant force. Good experiences will be governed less by the id (the pleasure component), and more by the super-ego (the more socially and morally conscious component). Bad experiences will tilt in the other direction with the ego allowing you to succumb to the forces of the id.

At the root of all of this psychology, or psychic apparatus, is the foundational assumption that our basic human drive is selfish-survival. This is known as the Darwinian-Freudian model of psychology. It essentially posits that humans are fundamentally no different than other creatures, since we have all evolved from the same ancestors. We all come from the same basic bacteria that evolved into all of the different species on earth. Darwin's theory of Natural Selection states that, variations within species are going to occur at random, and that the survival, or extinction of any organism, is based on its ability to adapt to change. And although Darwin didn't speak in psychological terms, it was Herbert Spencer, the British philosopher, who was the first person to use the term "Survival of the fittest," as the central pillar to "Social Darwinism," applying it to religion and society. Spencer used Darwin's arguments in Natural Selection to justify the colonization of much of the world by European forces. The argument was extended to the poor, being widely used to defend the unequal distribution of wealth at the time.

The parallels are made between the Darwinian Theory of Natural Selection in that survival of the fittest is the dominant force of nature, and thus the dominant force in man. The Darwinian-Freudian theory therefore fixates on this "Survival of the fittest," or attainment of pleasure, by man through the force of the id. This would suggest that the id is always the strongest force in man. There are variations to this theory, but this the general viewpoint that it conveys. Of course, this view is quite saddening, because it would essentially make for a lack of expectation in one another. If there were no rules to society, would we all just behave chaotically for the selfish-survival of the fittest? It's an interesting theory to say the least, but fortunately, we live in a society that is filled with rules. When we disobey the rules with misbehavior (i.e. break the law) we are punished. The rules of society are equitable to the mind's super-ego, whereas the id is the desire for man to gain pleasure regardless of those rules, while the ego acts as the police officer, or the moral compass. For some who can't seem to obey the rules, they are remanded repeatedly, and others have a strict adherence to the rules.

The behavior of any individual is a direct reflection of the behavior of the forces in his or her psychic apparatus. How a person behaves, indicates what forces are taking control at any given moment. Is he giving into pleasure, allowing the id to take over? Or, is he playing by the rules and being a pillar of society as the super-ego police officer weighs in? As the ego analyzes and weighs the pros and the cons of each decision, it ultimately reaches a verdict, which results in a particular type of behavior. The ego weighs decisions all the time, and has its own self-talk between the super-ego and id. However, the problem is that you're unaware of much of the self-talk since most of it happens in the subconscious mind. If you don't pay attention and build awareness, the ego can walk all over you.

If you allow the ego to reign supreme, you really will be a pawn in its chess game. While sometimes it may not be easy to tune into your own self-talk, you can tune into your body's emotions. Your body's emotions at any given moment are the radio station to your mind's antenna. As the self-talk occurs, you begin to feel different emotions –

thoughts are converted to emotions by the body, and your emotions are a direct reflection of what you're thinking. If you allow yourself to be aware of your emotions, and watch them, you can secretly discover what type of self-talk your psychic apparatus is having within the confines of your mind.

Since your inner beliefs are the foundation for your emotions, and resultant behaviors, if you can change your core beliefs that you have, and eradicate those hidden inner limiting beliefs your subconscious has, you can alter your behavior and better adapt to change. Of course, we all want to be able to eradicate our limiting behaviors. For some, it's easier said than done. If you can't build a keen awareness, and remove any toxins in your life, you will be unable to focus on honestly understanding your own behavior. If you can't understand your own behavior, you can't work to fix it, and properly pursue your hopes and dreams without letting your conundrum-filled psychic apparatus control your life.

ACTIONS SPEAK LOUDER THAN WORDS

Everyone has heard the phrase "Actions speak louder than words." It of course means that promises don't mean too much, but your actions do. The statement is generally used in trust exchanges, whether it's a trust in business, or trust in a personal relationship. Essentially this means that you can use your actions as an indication of your emotions. Since your actions are a direct extension of your emotions, which stem from your beliefs, and the self-talk in your mind, your actions indicate your true persona – and reigning force in your mind – far more than your words do. You might say you believe in one thing, but if your actions dictate otherwise, then clearly you don't.

So, what does this mean? Well, it's important to look at your actions anytime you're trying to make a change for the better. Whether you're just trying to adapt to your surrounding environment, make some lasting life changes, or truly move mountains, you have to understand why it is you do the things that you do, to get a better read on your true inner beliefs. Have you ever had a friend or been in a relationships with someone who says one thing but does the exact opposite? You know what I'm talking about, right? Most of us are guilty of doing this, but when it happens, it truly makes you stop and think. It can seem at times that a person may really want something, and they may themselves wholeheartedly believe that they do. However, when it comes down to it, they act in the exact opposite way, surprising even themselves. But the difficulty here is that the ego begins to make excuses for itself. They may say they want to quit smoking cigarettes, and really believe that they do, but it's clear from their actions that they are not 100% willing to do what it takes to quit, if they continue to keep smoking.

If this has happened to you, don't worry because you're not alone. Most people go through this, and although we may not want to admit it, it happens from time to time, but it's usually through the ego's infighting. We find ourselves being critical of others for things that we do because it's the ego's natural defense mechanism. And although we may say we don't like something, or that we do like something, when we do the opposite, the truth comes out. The infighting that occurs in your ego is oftentimes out of your control since so much of it occurs in the subconscious mind. Unless you have a keen awareness to this self-talk that's happening, it's hard to spot or control.

But spotting and controlling your self-talk is critical to accomplishing your goals, or achieving your hopes, and dreams, because these beliefs lie at the very heart of all that you do. Because you believe in a certain way, you act in a certain way. So, in order to understand what your true beliefs are, you have to look at your actions. For example, if you say that you want to make more money, yet, every chance you get extra time you spend it surfing the Web, watching television, or doing some other non-productive activity, you really don't want to make extra money that badly. You don't have the underlying belief that either you truly need to make more money, or want to. If it were a true belief, then you wouldn't procrastinate, but rather, you would make a plan and stick to it.

This applies to anything in life. When you see your actions going in the opposite direction of your intended goals in life, then those goals are not founded in enough deep-rooted beliefs for you to make them a reality. For example, Thomas Edison failed over 10,000 times to invent the light bulb. He failed so many times, but he kept trying, and he kept getting closer and closer to his goal. But, Edison believed, truly deep down inside, that he would invent the electric light bulb. He didn't have a doubt in his mind, and with each failure, he drew closer and closer to his goal. When Steve Jobs petitioned Apple to create the iPhone, he knew without a shadow of a doubt, that he would change the entire smartphone landscape with the new gadget, and he did. Apple failed many times to produce a working prototype for AT&T, but eventually they got it. And of course, that one phone changed the entire course of the company, which has now grown into one of the most valuable and trusted companies in the world. These were all the actions of people, and organizations, committed to a specific goal, which was founded on certain beliefs. Without these underlying, empowering beliefs, your own actions may run contrary to your conscious goals.

When Colonel Sanders, the founder of Kentucky Fried Chicken, set out at the age of 65 years old with just a chicken recipe, and a $105 social security check to his name, he believed – rather, he knew – that he would succeed. He knew, with certainty, that what he had was undeniably the best recipe for chicken anywhere, and he set out to create a franchise business when the model was still in its infancy. 1,009 separate chicken establishments turned him down. Can you imagine suffering that many rejections, setbacks, and failures, time and time again? But he knew – he believed – that he would succeed. He knew that what he had was better than gold, and his actions were proof of that.

There's something about having strong and powerful beliefs, but as you can see, the actions of these people spoke louder than words. It's important to look at your own actions. It's important to look at what you do on a daily basis, and whether its congruent with what you want in life. If you want to lose weight, are you making decisions that are congruent with a healthy lifestyle? Or, do you just want the instant gratification of weight loss, but not have to put in the hard work? These are very valid questions and help to really allow you to look inwards at your actions to indicate what type of infighting is going on in your ego.

It's not always your fault if you don't do as you say. A lot of it has to do with the emotional-numbing that the ego institutes in order to hide and protect our fragile inner selves. But the ego only exists in time – the ego dwells on the past, and envisions the future – but when you can be fully present, and aware of your thoughts and patterns, the ego can't hide from you. It can only shroud itself by using time as a camouflage, but if you pay very careful attention to your thoughts, your emotions, and your resultant actions, you can uncover the hidden beliefs residing deep in your subconscious mind. But this is only if you can be acutely aware and honest of your own behavior and actions. You have to watch yourself as a spectator would.

For example, have you ever found yourself drifting off, then being jarred back to reality – or the present moment – after having been in a train of thought that took you away from consciousness? Sure, you have. But the problem is that, although we tend to "drift off" like that from time to time, our mind does a lot of drifting that we're not aware of. With 60,000 thoughts running through your mind on a daily basis, your mind does a lot of thinking. That's many different thoughts that are being tossed around, analyzed, and deconstructed every day. That's a lot of decisions that are being made, conceptions that are being formed, and points of view being created. Since there is so much self-talk going on in the mind, if you're not acutely aware of what it is your mind is talking about with itself, it can spiral out of control. This is especially true for negative self-talk.

So, pay close attention to your actions, because they certainly speak louder than words. Use your actions, to help uncover your true beliefs. Act like an investigator and try to uncover what it is that you truly believe in. If you're acting contrary to what you think you believe in, what is it about that which makes you act that way? Usually, there's some hidden feeling inside that's buried that you don't have conscious access to. You have to search to find it. Search and be aware of what you're thinking of, because without doing that, your mind will run rampant and it will control you. You won't be able to accomplish those goals, pursue those hopes, or realize those dreams. You won't be able to move mountains when the molehills have infested your   mind.

5

THINKING POSITIVE

"Like success, failure is many things to many people. With Positive Mental Attitude, failure is a learning experience, a rung on the ladder, a plateau at which to get your thoughts in order and prepare to try again." – W. Clement Stone

Jennifer sat in front of her computer screen, fingers suspended in midair, her blog editing administration Webpage glaring back at her in front of her eyes. She was tired, and it was 2 o'clock in the morning. Her cat purred somewhere nearby. But Jennifer was still excited, even in the wee hours of the morning, pouring over her blog posts covering the span of one year. It was one year ago that she weighed over 100 pounds more than she did that day. It was one year ago that she decided to put all the pain, hurt, and rejection behind her. It was one year ago that she decided she would no longer allow herself to live a life in fear of food – she decided to become empowered.

Jennifer made herself a challenge. She challenged herself to lose 100 pounds within the span of one year, and she wasn't going to hide out anymore. No, Jennifer was going to let the world know about every single emotion that ran through her body on a particular day. She was going to let the whole world know how much she ate, what foods she put in her body, just how she felt, and how much she weighed. And she was going to do this *every single day*. She was going to do it no matter how hard it was going to be, because she was sick and tired of living a life filled with fear. She was tired of having to hide what she ate for fear that people would judge her. She was sick and tired of all the emotional pain, and anguish, she lived through every single day as a product of her childhood. Those feelings and emotions made her run back to the comfort of food. Food was her blanket. Food kept her warm at night – but not anymore.

She was done living that life, and a year ago, she vowed never again. She vowed she was going to think positively, and breed positivity. She knew it was going to be hard. She knew that her body would want to reject everything that she threw at it that was new and foreign. But she didn't care. She didn't care anymore about trying to cover up the pain. She was going to let herself free. She was going to let herself go. That was it. It was a promise.

She sat there at 2am, on the one-year anniversary of her big decision, fingers still suspended in mid-air, hovering over her keyboard, and her mind just wandered off. There was no medal awaiting her. There was no award to be collected. But there sure was some excitement in the blogosphere. There certainly were loads of comments and congratulations. She thought good and hard about what to write at that moment. She thought about how much she needed to thank all of her readers – she wanted to hug every single last one of them. They helped her through the tough times when she just wanted to retreat into the comfort of food. They were a Godsend to her. She couldn't be more thankful.

Her fingers touched the keys, and they were off. She began writing in a fury of words and sentences that she had become so accustomed to doing on a daily basis. She poured her heart out, thanking everyone for their support and their guidance. She felt blessed, but it all started with her. It all started with her utter belief in herself and the positivity that she surrounded herself with. She hung photos all over her room that inspired her – they were her fitness inspirations. She threw out clothing that was really oversized, and emptied her fridge and pantry of all the junk there was. She did all of that while blasting her iPod to the Queen song, "We are the Champions." That was a year ago, and she never looked back. But she was thankful. She was thankful for all the love and support. But she was the one that did it. She was the one that pulled it off. No one else did it for her. Somehow, she mustered up the state-of-mind to pull it off, and she succeeded. "Thank you," she said, mouthing the word as the rest of it spilled out of her and onto the screen in front of her. "Thank you. Thank you so much…"

*****

In a CNN interview with Piers Morgan, Anthony Robbins is quoted as saying, "The quality of your life is the quality of where you live emotionally." He went on to say, "But we all have a home. Angry people find a way to get angry even if their life doesn't have anything to be angry about. We can always find it. Sad people find a way to be sad. Caring people find a way to care for other people. So one thing to identify is where are you living? What's your home? What's your habit? And then the way to change it."

A lot of us tend to get set in our ways. We tend to think that the way we think is the only right way to think. If we have certain points of view, those points of view are the right points of view, and we'll argue vehemently against the opposing points of view. Even if we don't vocalize our arguments, we can hear the critical machine in our mind cranking and turning, spewing out arguments as to why the other side is wrong, and why what they're doing is right. We get set in our ways.

This happens to everyone. There's no little magic formula that you can run, that will allow you to sort out your own mental patterns and behaviors. Each person is unique, individual, and bases their beliefs on personal experiences, and the results of those experiences. If a person has had many "sad" experiences, then they've lived in a sad realm. Everything around them is seen with a sad kaleidoscope. Every comment, every action, every glance from another human being, makes them feel more sad in some way. Other people are happy. They live in that happy place, see things from a happy point of view, and walk down the street with a smile on their faces. They have a happy kaleidoscope.

But when you think about two separate people, and you think about the difference between someone who is sad, and someone who is happy, it begins to make you wonder. You wonder what makes that person so sad, or what makes that person so happy. You wonder how could two seemingly similar people, act so entirely different. If you've ever met that one person who always seems to be so happy and positive, you know what I'm talking about. There's something so contagious about them. You want to be like them; you wonder how they got to be so happy. Do they have the secret to it all?

Yet, still, most of us aren't very happy and don't think positive. Our mind tends to weigh the bad events of our lives more heavily on the scale of negativity. We begin to be critical and cynical about things in life. We just get jaded. We're all guilty of doing this at one point or another, but the problem is that most of us tend to let this get out of hand. We tend to look at things through the kaleidoscope of our very-biased mind, when in fact we should learn to have a more positive outlook on life.

I know what you're going to say – "If I pretend like nothing's wrong, I would be lying to myself." But, you're always going to have problems. Problems are a sign of life, and thinking positive doesn't mean that you need to ignore your problems. It just means that you should deal with your problems, but then learn to focus on the positive and good things in life. It means that you need to learn to have hope, even when things look bleak. You need to understand that there's a reason for it all. There's a reason why you have to go through so much struggle, and so much pain. Sometimes, the reason isn't so apparent right away. You have to get more distanced from the struggle and the pain before you can find the reasons, but they're there if you look.

You see, we're always going to have something to worry about. We're always going to have some sort of problems in our lives. But when you focus on the problems, and you focus on the negative, you'll only produce more problems, and more negativity. But if you focus on the positive, and the good in your life, then you'll get more good, and positivity. Oftentimes, it's hard to focus on the positive though. It's hard to look past that rut, or the present situation of events that led you to where you are today. But, you have to remember that there are people in far worse situations out there in life. You have to remember the types of struggles that people are going through, and how much pain and suffering there is. You have to remember to appreciate what you have in your own life. You need to find a sense of gratitude that will allow you to think more positive.

All too often, we tend to look to things that we don't have, as opposed to what we do have. We usually long for things, as opposed to being grateful for things. Life is a beautiful gift, and once you learn to happily succeed rather than succeeding to be happy, you will live a much fuller, stress-free life. You see, the mind is a very complex thing, yet it's also very basic in a way. If you look at the brain from a scientific point of view, you'll see this complex array of 80 to 100 billion neurons that form these vast neural networks of connections. When you have a thought, a neurotransmitter moves from one neuron to the next through gaps called synapses. Different neural networks, fire off for different functions of the mind and body. So, when you have a thought in your mind, a neural network of neurons comes to life, and begins a neurotransmission. That transmission includes sending and receiving neurotransmitters through neurons in the network of that particular thought. And all this complexity of neural networks allows you to conduct your thoughts, movements, and functions in your body and mind on a daily basis.

All of the thoughts and decision-making happening in your mind is either the product of your conscious thoughts, or your subconscious thoughts. There's also neurons working to help keep the systems of your body functioning, such as your heart, your lungs, your bladder, and so on. There's so much complexity in there that it's a marvel how it has all come together to produce this one living, breathing, organic machine called you. But aside from the complexity, you have the simplicity of your thoughts. A simple thought can spring so much to life in your mind. A simple thought could spark off a series of events that lead your mind to analyze a certain situation, or manifest a certain outcome. It all starts with a simple thought.

THOUGHTS ARE THINGS

There's something very powerful about the mind. In all of its complexity, there is something so simple. There's something simple that exists that, when conjured up, can spark off a firestorm of activity that can lead you to the very result you intended to achieve. "Thoughts are things." Yes, I remember when I first heard that quote I wasn't quite sure what to think of it. I wasn't quite sure what to think of the ability to take a simple thought and turn it into the result that I wanted. I was confused by how vividly holding a thought in your mind, could eventually manifest itself into reality. I was confused about all of this until I was able to prove to myself that thoughts certainly are things. I was able to prove that I could create the destiny of my dreams, by holding it vividly in my mind's eye, at the forefront of everything I did and was.

There's certainly more to the general concept of turning a simple thought into the result that you want, but your thoughts are where it all starts. It all starts with your capability to set your neural network ablaze with a thought, and implant it into both your subconscious, and conscious mind. So much goes on behind the scenes in your mind that one couldn't possibly fathom how thoughts actually become things. But, if you spend a bit of time just thinking about the interconnectedness of all things, in the physical and metaphysical spheres of life, you can begin to come to more of an appreciation of it. Thoughts travel through our mind across the gaps in neurons that exist in our brains. These billions upon billions of neurons are surrounded by neurochemicals that transmit these neurotransmissions. These are all connected in various clusters with ladder-like rungs. What's most incredible about this, is that all of this stemmed from evolution over hundreds of millions of years. Essentially, we all have the same microbial origins. The mass that makes up our bodies, and everything else on earth, are just atoms floating in space, clinging together through various electrical forces – forces we aren't even aware of that connect all things to one another.

This concept really started out in 1889 when a man by the name of Prentice Mulford published a book called, *Thoughts are Things*. Although it's been well over 100 years since the publishing of that book, it contains a lot of the modern thought movement material. Mulford was in fact, one of the founding fathers of the thought movement, and his book came well before books that touted the Law of Attraction and other modern day literary thought works. In his book, Mulford explains that we embody two different minds. There's the mind of the body, which is limited and fights external change, and there's the mind of the spirit, which is unlimited and offers the potential for the achievement of anything, and embraces external change.

Mulford explains that whatever it is we talk about, we attract to ourselves. If a group of people are talking about suffering and disease, then they attract that into their lives, and eventually bring disease and suffering in some form to themselves. But if there are a group of individuals talking about abundance, health, wealth, and positivity, then they will attract that into their lives. He also states that courage and the presence of mind mean the same thing, and that cowardice and the lack of mental control in one's self, also mean the same thing. And to have courage, you must have self-discipline. You must be able to focus on the here and now and avoid panic. It means a full awareness in the now and what you are doing, and not to be one that dwells in the past, or only wastes time wishing for the future.

The book is a powerful book for the thought movement, and many modern day motivational and inspirational books have been founded on the knowledge contained in this literary work. Books like *The Secret, The Power of Now, Think and Grow Rich,* and many others, use the concepts and principles taught in Mulford's work. It's incredible to note that even before modern science had discovered the complexities of how thoughts move through the mind, Mulford was able to write this book based on an analysis of his life and experiences. He was able to channel that spiritual cosmic knowledge that connects everyone and everything. Because, we are just all atoms that have been carefully arranged into matter, and all atoms are connected to one another on the earth. There's certainly something to say about having positive thoughts, and positive expectations. Your mind will reorganize things in your life to point you in the right direction. It's like having an internal roadmap to help achieve your goals, but if you don't think positive, you can't expect positive results.

Have you ever heard the saying, "The rich get richer, and the poor get poorer?" Of course, you have. Well, being rich, and being poor, is just as much a mentality of thought as anything else is. When Anthony Robbins said,

"The quality of your life is the quality of where you live emotionally," it was so very true. Essentially, they are all saying the same thing – Prentice Mulford, Anthony Robbins, and the cliché on the rich getting richer. They all involve certain thought patterns that build upon one another. The sad attract more sadness, the sick attract more sickness, the wealthy attract more wealth, the poor attract more poverty, and the happy attract more happiness. For some people, this is a difficult concept to grasp, but I can tell you from the experiences in my life, this has been 100% true. By steering your thoughts in the direction that you want to travel, you can change the trajectory of your life. If you've had obstacles, stop focusing and dwelling on those obstacles, and focus on the goal. You can move mountains when you focus on the goal, breed positivity, and live with positive expectations in life.

6
SEEING CLEARLY

"The key to growth is the introduction of higher dimensions of consciousness into our awareness." – Lao Tzu

The wet relentless rain pounded the vehicle that was plowing eastbound on the Long Island Expressway, pelting the grey mid-sized sedan like a heavy barrage of gunfire, leaving little visibility in its wake. The rain pelted the car like hundreds of small bullets ricocheting every second off the hollow steel frame of the rental car. The sound echoed violently inside the cabin, fraying the nerves of the two already weary travelers.

Campaigning through the treacherous weather conditions, Jon had to wince at times to see through the rain, just enough to make out the vehicles in front of him. The heaviest rainfall on record in the area made even the bright red glow of the car-filled highway's taillights, a dull-blurry haze. "It wasn't supposed to be like this. They didn't say it would be this bad." Jon shot a peripheral stare at his wife. The thick air of nervousness clung to the young couple like one of the ominous black clouds that was spewing rain in the sky above them.

"This is bad, Jon. This is bad." Stephanie stared straight ahead at the road in front of them as her thoughts raced a mile-a-minute.

Jon tried to keep it together. He steered the dark grey sedan down the middle lane of the partially flooded highway and nervously tried not to look affected by the atrocious weather before him. "I'm still glad we decided to do this. We needed to get away," he tried to make light of the situation.

"Get away? Jon, this rain is terrible."

"I know. I know."

"Maybe we should get off at the next exit and wait for the rain to die down." Stephanie, Jon's wife, looked at him for reassurance, searching his face, and analyzing the contorted looks he made as he tried to navigate the car across the chaotic lanes.

"No, we'll be okay. It's nearly dark and we still have a long way to drive." It was almost seven o'clock in the evening on the Friday before Easter. Their flight in from Chicago O'Hare airport had been delayed for just over three hours due to the incoming storm. The cold reception of dramatic weather, coupled with the delayed flight and stress of a full day of travel, heightened their already frayed nerves.

"You sure?" She shot him another nervous glance then turned her head to look out the window, at the passing scenery that was barely visible through the rain. She watched through blurred vision as the forest-like evergreens that encased the highway zipped past them, as they pushed towards their destination.

"Don't worry." Jon gripped the grey laminate steering wheel of the rental car tighter than he had ever gripped a steering wheel before in his life. White-knuckled, and hands glued at 10 and 2 o'clock, he kept driving and navigating the car through the torrential deluge. Only the wiper blades that squeaked violently, as they made feeble attempts to wipe the ceaseless rain off the windshield, broke the silence in the vehicle.

"I'm worried."

"Don't be." Jon steadied the wheel as the car lost its traction and regained it again for the tenth time. He was nervous, but he tried to appear confident. He had been through worse weather, and he wasn't about to loose his cool now.

"Jon, please." She gave him a long glare. She had always trusted her husband and his judgment, so she tried to keep her cool, but it was weighing on her.

"If they had given us the SUV we asked for in the first place, then there wouldn't have been a problem. Remind me to call and complain when we get home."

"I just can't believe the one day we decide to travel, we have to deal with this." She waved her hands out in front of her, palms up, indicating the sketchy scene out in front of them. She was beginning to lose her cool, and it was showing. An alarm was sounding inside her head, but she wasn't sure how to turn it off. The incessant beeping that only she could hear was making it hard for her to stay inside her skin.

"Look, we'll get there soon enough. Besides, this rain

will have to let up at some point." Jon couldn't see, but he was still trying to play it cool while he cocked his head downwards in a futile attempt to see under the rain. Their three-year-old daughter was in the back seat wearing a pair of fuzzy pink headphones while watching cartoons on a portable DVD player.

"Jon. Please, stop the car and let's get off the highway. I have a really bad feeling about this." She glanced over, this time almost half held her breath as a late model sports car swerved in front them, losing control, then regaining it. "Watch out for that car, he's driving like a lunatic!" She nearly jumped out of her seat as she pointed and screamed, peaking the attention of their daughter. The ferocious rain made it difficult to see anything. "Are these people mad?"

"Maybe they're just used to this kind of weather or maybe this is just how they always drive in New York." Jon's feeble attempt at a joke didn't work.

"How can they be used to this kind of weather? This is extreme. You can barely see anything." Stephanie's voice was trembling.

It's okay. Stop worrying. Relax..." his voice trailed off, you could hear the nervousness embedded in the very fibers of his words.

Even for spring in the northeast, it was cold, unseasonably cold, and the rain wasn't letting up. The cold front that had hit the area that afternoon made it feel like it was still winter – it was the kind of cold that oozed into your skin, right down to the bone. It was far too cold for that time of year.

Jon still could hardly see through the incessant rain hitting the windshield. They hit a patch of misty fog, and the visibility dropped down even further. "Jon, this weather is so strange, how can it be this cold in April? It feels like it's below freezing out there." Jon just tried to shrug it off. It was the Northeast after all, and it was prone to unpredictable weather at times.

"We'll get there soon, we're not too far, another couple hours in these conditions and we should... we'll get there." Jon knew they would get there, but he wasn't sure how long it would take. As he was speaking, his wife unbuckled her seatbelt, and reached back to grab their daughter's toy that had fallen just out of her grasp in front of her. Jon diverted his attention to eye the fallen toy just behind the passenger's seat.

"Sweetheart, hang on a second, let me grab that for you."

Then it happened. The late model sports car reappeared, swerving out of control right in front of an 18-wheeler, its tires slipping and catching over and over, as it tried to regain traction while slamming on its breaks hard. Jon's diverted attention arrived back to the picture unfolding in front of him, with the sports car careening towards them from the right, towards the center divider. Jon swerved the car, first to the left to avoid the oncoming sports car while narrowly missing it, then to the right, straight towards the semi truck that was losing control in an effort to avoid the car that had almost hit it.

The sports car regained traction, its rear end thrashing violently, and then sped off leaving Jon fighting tirelessly to regain control of his vehicle. He swerved the sedan again to the left to avoid the semi truck this time, spinning and buckling the rear wheels while hydroplaning across the highway. Pressing down hard on the breaks to try to avoid the car in front of him, then jamming the wheel in the other direction, the vehicle lunged forward spinning violently.

It all happened in an instant. Stephanie's seatbelt was unbuckled trying to get the toy that fell on the ground for Rebecca, while Jon was fighting to get control of the wheel, which was now next to impossible to do, and everything came undone at that moment. In a violent spin across the highway towards the semi truck, *time seemed to stand still while every excruciating detail occurred in slow motion.*

*****

Have you ever been faced with a life-threatening situation? I mean, have you ever come face to face with death, or had a near-death experience? What is it about situations of incredible amounts of danger, or the potential of death, that makes your senses come alive? If this has ever happened to you, then you know just what I'm talking about. There's something about these types of situations, which draws you into the present moment – when they happen, nothing else matters. All of a sudden, your senses come alive, and you're acutely aware of what's going on. Things tend to even go in slow motion, in the case of bad accidents for example. Things just slow down, and it's almost as if life becomes a stop-motion picture frame of stills.

This is probably one of the most surreal experiences that you can ever have. When life comes grinding to a near halt, and things begin happening in slow motion, something peculiar begins to happen. You have no concept of time at that moment. You're not thinking about the past or the future. All you're concerned about is the present moment – the *now*. Although no one wants to go through these types of situations, something happens to you when you do. It's almost as if an internal shift occurs –

an awakening if you will. You instantly feel alive. I'm not talking about the kind of alive that you feel right now, wherever you may be reading the words on this page, I'm talking about a different kind of alive. I'm talking about the kind of alive that doesn't involve a sense of time. You're not concerned with what happened yesterday, or even what's going to happen tomorrow. You're only concerned about what's happening *right now*.

If you've ever experienced this, it's exhilarating. Unfortunately, however, this is one of the few times in life that people ever really do feel alive. Why is that? It's because most people are so caught up living in either the past, or the future, so much that they forget about the present moment. They are so concerned with what happened to them years, months, or even days ago, that it consumes all of their mental capacity. It disallows them from focusing on the now, and feeling truly alive. Why is the now important? Well, your ego lives in the realm of time. Meaning that the ego knows past and future, it doesn't know present – it can't exist in the now. If you focus on the now, and the present moment in time, you can move mountains. When you become so fixated on past disappointments, or you're only waiting for some future achievement, you can't be free right now. When you're free right now, you can truly live, and you can accomplish anything in the now. It's only a state of mind.

Happiness lives in the now. People that are happy, are present, and are able to focus on the present moment rather than be caught up in the past events of their lives. There's something powerful about focusing on the now. For example, take the room that you're sitting in, or the space that you're occupying right now. What color are the walls? If you're outside, what's nearby? If you're near some grass, are there flowers near the grass? If you're inside, are the lights on? If so, what kinds of lights are on? Can you feel the energy coming from the lights? How does that feel to you? Can you hear the buzzing of the lights, or the chirping of birds in the distance? I mention these because, all too often, we don't pay attention to the details in our lives. We don't see the beauty of things that surround us. But, when something very bad happens, we come back down to earth and begin appreciating the beauty in our lives. If someone we love or care about went through a health scare, a bad accident, or a near-death experience, and you yourself haven't, ask him or her how things felt afterwards. Ask them how much they began to take an appreciation for all things in their lives afterwards.

When you're pursuing your goals, and your dreams, and you're trying to move mountains, you have to be present and live in the now. When you begin to fixate yourself on all the past errors and failures of your life, you lose alignment with the present moment and the now. It's hard for some people to really let go of the past, but if you want to accomplish your goals, and fulfill your dreams, you have to live in the now. You can't live in the past, and you can't just only hope for the future. It's okay to acknowledge the past events of your life, but they don't matter in the now. They don't matter in the present moment of time, and in the beauty of the life that you lead. It doesn't matter what you don't have, it matters what you do have. It doesn't matter how much hurt, or pain you've been through, what matters is the appreciation for what you've learned, what you've gained, and what you have right now. Let go of the past, or it will continue to limit you. Let go of the pain, the hurt, and the rejection. So many people in the world have so little and can still find some source of happiness by being present in the now. You shouldn't only base your life on the attainment of things, or solely on the disappointments or pain of your past, but rather, on your capability to be open and aware of the present moment in time.

If you've ever heard the saying, "There's no time like

the present moment," it's so very true. There certainly is no time like the present moment – there's no time like the now. So much can happen in the present moment. You can instantly make a decision that will alter the shape of the rest of your life. You can instantly make a decision that will push you towards your hopes and your dreams. You can instantly make a decision to let go of the past hurt and the pain, and truly begin to live your life right now. You can instantly make a decision that will eventually lead you to move those mountains, and accomplish anything your heart desires. There's no time like the now. The present moment is what matters. You can focus and plan your goals for long enough that it takes to be aware of time-based things, but come back to the present moment and live in the now, and you can accomplish anything.

Some people might not agree with these statements. Some people might say that they need to think about the past and the future because it's what's defined them. Yes, this is true, but the present is more important. When you live in the present, you don't allow your ego to reign supreme. It can only take over when you allow yourself to live in the past and the future. When you begin to only dwell on events of the past, or only dwell on your hopes for the future, you can't live in the now. This isn't to say that you're supposed to forget about time altogether. Time is important for its practical applications, because modern day life revolves around time, but time is inconsequential. Consciousness of the now is what's important.

There's another important aspect to living in the now. Anytime you have self-deprecating and self-limiting beliefs, the only way to truly uncover and eradicate them is by using your consciousness of the now. Remember the discussion of the ego and how the different parts interact with one another? Well, some of that interaction is subconscious and some of it is conscious. But, when you can be very conscious of the interaction, although you still won't hear the subconscious talk, you will hear the negative self-talk that's in the conscious realm of your mind. And, even when you don't hear the subconscious talk, your emotions will signal what's going on in your mind, as long as you can be present enough, and aware, in the now, you can uncover the subconscious self-talk as well. Your emotions are the gateway to your thoughts, and those emotions signal us to act in certain ways.

So, if your thoughts in your subconscious mind are filled with fear, anxiety, and worry, you're going to feel those emotions and act in a certain way. But, when you can stop, and be aware of what's going on in your own mind, and you can pay careful attention to it, you can replace those negative thought patterns with positive ones. This takes a lot of practice, and the supplanting of positive affirmations. Because your negative self-talk has been installed and upgraded in your mind over the years, as you've dwelled on the negative aspects of your life, this will take some work. But with consistent effort, you can replace the negative with the positive if you stay focused, and you stay present. Remember, thoughts are things, and what you focus on you will bring into reality. This is not going to happen overnight, but like a plant that grows from a small seedling to a towering and tall tree with deep roots, positive thoughts will eventually take root and blossom. Focus your mind on positivity, move in that direction, and be conscious of your thoughts and emotions.

By entering into the present moment, and being fully aware, you can pay witness to the negative self-talk that your ego has with your inner self. When you can catch it in this negative loop, you can build an understanding of your mind and how it operates, and work to stop it dead in its tracks. The negative self-talk is normal though, because it happens to all of us. It's a defense mechanism erected by the mind, but unfortunately, it does more to hurt us than to help us. It holds us back in life, keeps us quiet and subdued. And it bases many of its decisions on fear – fear of the unknown, fear of getting hurt, general anxiety and worry. All of this is grounded in your subconscious mind, and your level of fear will vary depending on your past experiences, and the types of beliefs that have been instilled in your mind over the years. But, don't let your mind's negativity defeat you and limit you. Br present, be aware, and work on stopping it dead in its tracks.

CREATING INNER BELIEF AWARENESS

It's okay to have goals and dreams that may be outside your realm of what you might have thought was possible at one point in your life. It's okay to expand your vision and pursue big things, no matter what type of adversity you're faced with. But it's not okay to allow yourself to be continuously limited by your hidden inner beliefs, created by your ego. These are the self-deprecating, self-limiting beliefs that will hinder you, not help you. These are the types of beliefs that you need to eradicate, because if you don't, you'll find yourself throwing in that towel and saying, "I give up."

It's difficult to spot these inner beliefs, which is why so many people are frustrated when they attempt to do things like lose weight, quit smoking, quit drinking, or jump on board a get-rich-quick scheme. Most people easily falter at the slightest sign of resistance. They give up because their inner beliefs, created by their egos, allow them to do so. When you can't live in the present moment, and be fully aware, it's difficult to uncover these hidden inner beliefs. You can't uncover the voices in your head – the voices that keep ringing out and telling you that you're not good enough, smart enough, or passionate enough to achieve something in your life. You can't abolish those words that spread like a fungal infection, infecting all the neurons in the subconscious, as it's allowed to propagate, uninhibited in the deep and far reaches of your mind.

You have to create inner belief awareness by uncovering all of the ego's hidden agendas. Yes, they are hidden agendas, because they serve to limit you, they don't serve to help you. They serve to limit you because the ego thinks that by harboring these inner beliefs, it's giving you more pleasure than pain. It's giving you more pleasure because, it knows you're going to come back to the hidden inner beliefs that you'll need as a crutch. Things like "More money, more problems," "I don't have a drinking problem," "I can stop smoking whenever I want. I just don't want to stop right now," "I'm just big boned," or "I didn't really want that job anyways," all help to mask the inner hurt that's on the inside. They just help to protect that very fragile inner part of you. As you can see, it's just the body's defense mechanism, and it's part of the "selfish survival," of our race. The ego can't find anything wrong with itself, because that wouldn't serve it. Why do you think it's next to impossible to get drug addicts to see what they're doing wrong, or criminals to be rehabilitated? Yes, those are extreme examples, but what about the shopaholics who use the emotion-numbing experience of buying and spending to mask dealing with what's on the inside? Same thing applies to food for overweight people, cigarette smoking, alcoholism, and everything in between.

All of our problems that we have, started out as ways to mask our hurt and fragile inner selves, and engage in emotion-numbing activities that the ego would rather make you do, than deal with the pain on the inside. Remember, it's trying to avoid pain and gain pleasure, and once you start coming to an understanding of just what great lengths your own ego will go to, in order to help "protect" you, you'll understand the severity of the situation. You have to uncover these inner beliefs, and you have to rid yourself of all the emotion-numbing activities that make you avoid dealing with the pain on the inside. It's okay to have pain. It's okay to have failure. Don't run from it – face it and deal with it. Conquer it. Everyone in life is faced with pain and failure in some form. But, the more you run from it, the more you will engage in emotion-numbing activities, and the less you will do to strive towards your outward hopes, dreams, and goals. You won't be able to move mountains, when all you're doing is trying to mask the pain on the inside.

This is the most difficult part of goal setting. This is why we have so many fad diets, and get-rich-quick schemes. People think they want something, but they want it fast – they want instant gratification. But, what they don't understand is that, they will always fail if they don't deal with their hidden inner beliefs first. Once the instant gratification turns into something that seems like it's going to take more work than they thought, the ego kicks back in and pushes them towards endeavors that are more pleasurable. It pushes them towards the emotion-numbing activities that they've become so accustomed to. It will always do this, unless you deal with it. You have to eradicate those limiting inner beliefs, and deal with your emotional pain. This is so very important.

7

SETTING GOALS

"Our goals can only be reached through a vehicle of a plan, in which we must fervently believe, and upon which we must vigorously act. There is no other route to success." – Pablo Picasso

Over a hundred years ago, an Army General led his troops to battle. They landed ashore with dozens of ships, disembarked, and the troops gathered on the shoreline awaiting commands from the General. The General looked at his men, and paced up and down the shoreline. He saw some of them with determined looks, but most others had a look that didn't quite sit right with him. They didn't look committed to winning the battle. "Men," he said, "today we face an enemy far superior to us. We face an enemy that is stronger, faster, and more capable than us. They outnumber us two to one, and as I stand here on this shore looking at you all, I am not quite convinced we will win this battle. I am not quite convinced that you men have the spirit, and the courage, to defeat the enemy here today. Are you real men, or are you cowards? All I see are cowards in front of me."

As the men listened to the Army General speaking, they continued to look on quietly, listening to the old man commanding his Army in his rant-like fashion. However, the men weren't convinced that they could win the battle, and that was abundantly obvious. There was a clear look of silent resignation on some of their faces. Were they cowards? The men started thinking of the severity of the situation that they faced. They thought about the severity of the enemy and the superiority of its forces. They were certainly faster, stronger, and more capable of winning the battle, which they had home field advantage for. After a few moments of thought by the troops, the Army Captain stepped forward and asked to address the General. "Sir, may I speak?"

"Yes, you may."

"Sir, we are outnumbered, outgunned, and are in foreign territory. How do you expect us to win this battle? We are but barely one thousand men, yet we face an enemy with fortified walls that can reign down fire and brimstone from above. We don't have enough archers, we don't have enough men, and we don't have enough weaponry to win."

The statement from the Army Captain disappointed the General, but it was as he had expected. He continued pacing up and down the shoreline until he got an idea. "Men," he said, "what is it that's most important to you in life? What is it that you would live and die for?" He knew the answer wouldn't be country, because if it were, those men would have been motivated enough to fight beyond anything he could have ever asked for.

"One by one, the troops started calling out their answers."

"Family," said the Army Captain.

"For my son, General. For my son I would do anything," said another troop who had stepped forward.

"For the love of my five children," said yet another troop, who also stepped forward. "For the love of my children I would do anything. I would go anywhere, fight anyone, and persevere through anything."

"For my wife and children I too would do anything," said the Army Captain, "I think most of these men would, which is why it's suicide for us to continue into a battle that we will surely lose. It's suicide for each and ever soldier standing on this shoreline, at this very moment. And they all know that it's suicide. For us to win would be next to impossible."

After the Army Captain had spoken, the General continued pacing the shoreline. Yes, he had heard all that he needed to hear. He pulled aside several of his Lieutenants, and made a decision. He was going to burn all the ships.

The Lieutenants cast great balls of fire onto the ship decks, and the Army's soldiers stood on the shore of the ocean watching the ships as they burned. They stood there in a sense of total misbelief of what they were seeing. They could no longer retreat. There was no turning back now. The only way for them to get back home was to invade, march straight through the city, and back north towards their homes.

"Sir? But, how will we return now?" asked the Army Captain.

"Ah, now, you have no choice but to fight. You have no choice now but to win this battle. The ships are burned, and there is no turning back. If you love your family as much as you say you do, then you will do whatever it is in your power to win this battle, and conquer this city. If you don't, you will never see your families again." The General looked on the faces of the soldiers, which had turned to stone. The looks of desperation were gone, and they were replaced with looks of determination. Each of the men was determined to now win the battle and conquer the city, in order to return home to the families they loved. Now, they had no choice.

*****

Sometimes in life, you have to burn the ships, so to speak. This analogy is an important one when it comes to accomplishing any major goals, or dreams. When you burn the ships, you have no point of return other than to accomplish the goal. For some people, this is the only way that they can succeed. By leaving themselves no alternatives, they persevere. It's a do-or-die situation, sink-or-swim, and there's no turning back. There's no going back and undoing that decision, and when it comes to accomplishing major feats, and goals in life, sometimes you just have to burn the ships. Sometimes you just have to leave yourself no other alternative.

Burning the ships is a strategy that works because your selfish-survival instinct kicks in. We do whatever is necessary in order to survive, because it's in our genetics. When an Army General burns the ships with no hopes of retreat, the troops' mood suddenly changes. That's because they've just switched into survival mode. Survival is also the mode you go into in order to pay your rent or your mortgage, your car payment, and put food on your plate. You have to have money to survive, and some people use this concept to sink or swim. When a son or a daughter moves out of the family home on their own, without a job to help support themselves, they have to survive. They have no choice, especially if they feel like they don't have anyone to fall back on. You will always do more to avoid pain than you will to gain pleasure, and not surviving is the worst amount of pain your body can experience. It will do anything to fight to stay alive, and get you through things because it's in its instinctive nature to do so.

But this concept doesn't work for everyone. Not everyone can venture out and burn the ships for no return. Not everyone can conjure up all that it takes to succeed. But once they have no other choice, as in there are no family or friends to support them if they fall flat on their faces, they usually make it work. Just imagine it for a moment. If you've ever been in a similar situation where you had to survive, and you had no other choice, that's just what you did – you survived. But in light of having to burn all the ships, and destroy any source of retreat, if you can build your goals up to have a strong enough meaning for you then you can also overcome any obstacle. Your ego will revert you back to emotion-numbing activities when a goal doesn't mean that much to you.

You have to have a strong enough meaning, that's deep-rooted, for you to conquer those goals, and move those mountains. Anything in life worthwhile, takes a significant amount of effort, and for some, that effort can only come about when they leave themselves no other choice. Of course, when you have no other choice, there's an enormous meaning for you to survive. But aside from having no other options, when you're trying to make some sort of voluntary change, or achieve some goal in your life that's worth pursuing, you have to attribute a strong enough meaning to it. If you can do that, and you can eradicate those hidden inner beliefs that may limit you, then you can do just about anything – then you can move mountains. But without meaning behind it all, most people throw in the towel in silent resignation and give up. Those troops would have given up very quickly had they had a method for retreat.

And like an Army set to wage battle, you must have a strong enough reason why you want to achieve your goals. You must have a strong enough reason why you won't ever turn back and quit. No matter what it is that you want in life, you have believe that you can achieve it. You have to believe that you can attain success, no matter what. In the face of all adversity, no matter what obstacles are thrown in your way, you are going to achieve the success that you want in your life. Without a strong positive mentality, and strong enough meanings to back up your goals - along with the belief that you can overcome anything – you won't succeed. You won't succeed when it comes to goals involving voluntary change, unless you do that.

SETTING GOALS FOR SUCCESS

At the heart of achieving the success that you want in life, is goal setting. Without the simple skillful art of goal setting, and doing it properly, you can't achieve the things that you want to achieve in life. This is especially true when it comes to achieving major voluntary changes in your life. I'm not talking about having to adapt to or overcome involuntary change; I'm talking about the kind of change that makes you a better person. I'm talking about the kind of change that lets you move mountains.

When you actually set your goals, and put pen to paper, or words to the screen, something happens inside of you. Those thoughts that manifest themselves on paper in front of you, all of a sudden come to life. They materialize, and you get to see them right there in front of your mind's eye, staring back at you. They all of a sudden become more real. There's something visceral about setting goals on paper. It's much different than doing it in your head. If you want to overcome your obstacles, and truly move mountains, you have to set pen to paper. You have to actually write out those goals and create an action plan. Thoughts are things, and those thoughts come to life, the more detail you add to them. The more you can envision them, and why you believe you must achieve them, the more likely you will be able to do so. The less you envision, plan, and strategize, the less likely you'll be to achieve them.

The tools that I've discussed up until now are critical to achieving the successes in life that you want – they are vital in your ability to move mountains. When we talk about being able to achieve anything using the power of positive thinking, it's truly as real as anything can get. Of course, that positive thinking needs to have some fuel behind it. It needs to be fueled with action, but to even get to that place you need to build the awareness in your ego for things that may be limiting you. You need to try to understand why you do the things that you do. Why do you constantly live with negative self-talk? Why do you say you want something, yet when it comes time to get to work, you slack off?

It happens to everyone, but if you're truly committed to designing a life that will be fruitful, and filled with achievement, you have to do the work. You have to be willing to make the sacrifices, work those long hours, and toil away endlessly. You can't think about the failures of the past, or dread the work required in the future, you just have to be present in the now and just do it. You have to grind away to get it done. It's that plain and simple. And when it comes to setting your goals on paper, you have to ensure that you follow through with some simple planning to clarify what those goals mean to you, and what reason you have for wanting to achieve them.

In life, all of us have goals. Some have lofty and

grandiose goals, while others have more subtle goals. But no matter what your goals in life are, they have to have meaning to you. They truly need to indicate something important that's near and dear to your heart. Some people achieve goals for their families, other do it for security, some for freedom, and others for country. Whatever your reasons are, they have to be strong. They have to be so strong that no matter how many times you fail, you get back up and try again. No matter how many times you face adversity, you persevere. That's how you set goals because without that – without actually placing that on paper in front of you – you'll end up giving up.

We all give up in life on things some of the time. We all throw in the towel from time to time, but if you've ever been in a situation where you didn't give up, you had a strong reason why you *had to succeed*. It was a "must" for you, it wasn't a "should." When goals are just a "should," they don't work. They don't work, because when the going gets tough, the tough just quit. That's because the ego steps in, and replays that emotion-numbing activity for you, so that your fragile inner self doesn't get hurt. It allows the id to win, tipping the scale in its favor. Remember, you have to be able to overcome that negative self-talk, otherwise, you won't be able to achieve you goals, and move those mountains.

There's a right way to set goals, then there's a wrong way to set goals. If you set goals the right way, then the likelihood of achieving them skyrockets. But, if you engage in the more passive goal setting that's become akin to most people's lives, then your chances of achieving them will not be so good. To really achieve your goals, you have to actively set them. What does this mean? Well you have to write them down for starters. You have to put that pen to paper, or fingers to the keyboard and get to work. As you set your goals, you have to be very specific. You have to know exactly what you want and when you want to achieve it by. Remember, you can't be too specific here. The more specific you are, the better.

So how does this work? Well, the goal here is to accomplish something major right? The goal here is to overcome some obstacle, or accomplish some life long hope or dream, and move that mountain, isn't it? If you've tried in the past to set goals, and you failed, for starters, it's because you didn't set them the right way. Of course, there's more to achieving the goals than just setting them the right way, but actively setting your goals the right way is a prerequisite to achievement. When you set goals the right way, and you actively have them clear on paper and in your mind, something just clicks for you. You know what direction you're steering the car called your life. When you veer off course, you know that you've done so, and if you plan right, you know what you need to do to get back on track. That's what active goal setting is. It involves being actively involved in the goal; it's not something that you're passive about. It's not something that just stays in your mind with some distant hope or dream. No, it has to be visceral and real, always in front of you so that your subconscious can reorganize your life, your actions, and your deeds, to help to steer you towards that goal. Whatever you focus on, you will get, and if you focus on your goals, and you don't give up, eventually you will reach them.

But overall, there really are three major components to active goal setting and achieving your goals, and those are:

1. **Be extremely specific about your goals** – When I mean be specific, I mean be extremely specific. What do you want in life? When do you want it by? What's your game plan to achieve the goal? You need to write out a very specific description

of your goal, and the date you want to attain it by, and why the goal is so important to you. If you have money goals, then you have to be very, very specific. How much money do you want? When do you want it by? Why do you want it so badly? Do you have weight loss goals? How much weight do you want to lose *exactly*? When do you want to lose it by? Split those goals up into milestones. If you want to lose 50 pounds in 6 months, break the goal apart into monthly, weekly, and even daily goals. See just what you need to do in a day to achieve that goal, and shoot for it. Focus on the present, don't dwell on the past, and don't allow yourself to give up.

2. **Tracking your goals** - Besides for being very specific about your goals, you need to be able to track your goals. Any successful goal setter knows that the analytics and tracking of their goals is critical to their overall success. This is where computer and tablet spreadsheets come in very handy. Make yourself a spreadsheet and track your daily progress. Because, when you can track your daily progress, it provides you with a more realistic understanding of where you are, versus where you need to be. It can also be very uplifting by looking at where you were days, weeks, or months ago, versus where you are today.

3. **Steering in the right direction** – The last major component of active goal setting is to always ensure that you're steering in the right direction. For example, a plane takes off from Hawaii, headed towards Miami and it charts its course to

land at the Miami International Airport. That plane has a goal. Along the way, it may steer off course to avoid turbulence, a storm, or other airplanes that may have been charted to cross paths with it. So, the pilots make adjustments as they go along, modifying their route. But the goal still stays the same. The goal remains to land at Miami International Airport. You must actively monitor, and steer yourself in the right direction, on a daily basis, towards the attainment of your goals.

Don't become a passive goal setter. You won't be able to move mountains by setting passive goals. Make them active, and take to pen and paper, or put words to the screen. Make a specific action plan of the goals you want to achieve, and come up with a strong enough reason why you want to achieve each of them. These goals have to mean something to you. They have to mean something deep and profound. They have to be so important to you, that no matter what, you'll never be able to turn back. You'll stay committed to them even in the face of failure.

8

HOW TO MOVE MOUNTAINS

"Success is not final, failure is not fatal: it is the courage to continue that counts." – Winston Churchill

Your ability to accomplish anything in life boils down to your beliefs. If you believe you can accomplish something, then you can. But, I'm not talking about half-hearted beliefs, I'm talking about having every cell in your body wholeheartedly believe and drive towards a goal. If you can believe deeply enough in your ability to accomplish something, you will. There's been nothing more powerful in history, than man's belief in what he can accomplish. More progress has been made in the past 100 years, than has happened in all of humanity. It's not just about survival. Yes, survival is necessary, but once we've accomplished the necessities for survival, people want to thrive. People want to thrive and provide a better, and more comfortable life, for themselves, and their loved ones. Survival is instinctive – it's laced in our genetic code – but it's the desire to thrive, that's born into our spirits as we come of age. It's thriving that keeps the wheel of progress turning and spinning, faster and faster.

All too often, however, people just are caught up in survival mode. They allow life's difficulties to weigh them down, and begin to focus on the negative. If this has resembled your past before, you have to make a decision right here, and right now that you'll never do this again. In an instant, a decision can be made. All it takes is an instant. All it takes is just one instant to say, "Never again." Never again will you put up for a life of mediocrity, of dwelling in the past, or solely hoping for the future. No, it's time right now that you start living. It's time to start living your life, and expecting good things to come. You must expect, and envision, a positive future for yourself. You must expect good things to happen to you. If you focus on the negative, only the negative will come along. Keep your eye on positivity, acknowledge the negative, but don't allow it to consume you. Keep your eye on the prize, and be positive, and you will reap positivity.

But aside from being positive, setting your goals, and coming to a deep and profound understanding of your ego, and your true inner self, there's one last ingredient to success. There's one last ingredient to succeeding at any goal, accomplishing any hope, or achieving any dream. There's one last ingredient for moving mountains – massive action. If you can take massive action, and do it on a daily basis, little by little you will chip away at your obstacles. You will chip away each, and every single day, and like the stonecutters, you will eventually make progress towards your dreams. You will eventually build your own cathedral. You will eventually fulfill your hopes, your dreams, and your desires. You will eventually move mountains.

Moving mountains doesn't happen overnight. Moving mountains doesn't come easy either. It takes work. It takes a lot of work to make the kind of progress required to move mountains. No matter what it is, your solution is never going to be a quick fix. You have to stick it out, whatever it is. If it truly means something to you, then you need to fight for it. You can't give up. You can't succumb to life, and all its pressures, by cracking under the weight of it. Many people have come before you, and many people will come after you, all of whom have pushed, and pushed, in the face of great adversity. They failed, over, and over again, but they kept getting back up. They didn't allow themselves to succumb to failure. They didn't allow the hurt and the pain of a failure to limit them. No, they got back up; they did it again, and again, and again, until they succeeded.

Life can be hard. Life can be very hard at times, and it can throw you curveballs. Not everything is going to go the way that you plan it to go. Not everything is going to turn out just how you would like it to turn out. But, that's why we adapt. We adapt to change that's involuntary, but in order to move mountains in life, you must adapt to change that's voluntary. You must be able to have the will, and the spirit, to adapt to anything you set your hopes on. You must be able to adapt to any change that occurs in the pursuit of your hopes, and your dreams. Whether it be emotional, physical, spiritual, mental, financial, or anything else, you must adapt to thrive. You must adapt to voluntary change in order to thrive. Survival is a necessity, but thriving is a desire that we all have – it's part of the flame of hope, which we all keep, lit alive in our hearts, always and forever. Human beings were made to thrive; not just survive. It's time you get to thriving, and not just surviving. It's time you "say to that mountain, 'Move from here to there,' and it will move. Nothing will be impossible for you."

OTHER BOOKS IN THIS SERIES

Thank you for taking the time to read this book. I truly hope that you enjoyed it, and I would like to take a moment of your time to share your thoughts with the online community by posting a review on Amazon. If this book inspired you in any way, shape, or form, I would love to hear about it in a book review. You can find the Amazon Book page located at the following URL - http://www.amazon.com/dp/B00D3MKVH4.

I put a lot of care into the books that I write and I hope that this care and sincerity come across in my writing because in the end I write to bring value to other people's lives. I hope that this book has brought some value to your life. I truly do.

This book is the sixth book in the *Inspirational Books Series* of personal development books that I've released. You can check out the other books in the series that are available as well, in the proceeding list:

- *How Not to Give Up* – *A Motivational & Inspirational Guide to Goal Setting & Achieving your Dreams (Volume 1)*

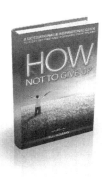

- *The Silk Merchant* – *Ancient Words of Wisdom to Help you Live a Better Life Today (Volume 2)*

- *Have a Little Hope* – *An Inspirational Guide to Discovering What Hope is and How to Have More of it in Your Life (Volume 3)*

- *Breakthrough* – *Live an Inspired Life, Overcome your Obstacles, and Accomplish your Dreams*

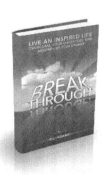

- *How to Be Happy* – *An Inspirational Guide to Discovering What Happiness is and How to have More of it in your Life*

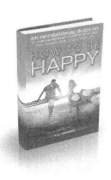

Made in the USA
Lexington, KY
22 September 2013